A Close World Apart

By

B. Thomas Kattapuram

ISBN: 1-4140-0189-4 (e-book)
ISBN: 1-4140-0190-8 (Paperback)

Library of Congress Control Number: 2003098165

This book is printed on acid free paper.

Printed in the United States of America
Bloomington, IN

1stBooks - rev. 11/14/03

For Amma, Achayan and Maseru.

For all the memories.

CHAPTER 1

Mammen's Journey

"Shit, I don't have time for this," complained the burly, bespectacled black visa officer as he ruffled through the papers in front of him.

Mammen kept quiet, avoiding direct eye contact, but making sure his body language did not betray his fear, as he stood in front of the officer.

"How's this...your pay stub does not add up to your annual salary," commented the officer tapping the pay stub with a pencil in a manner that people do when they show they have proved something.

"Sir, if you multiply seventeen fifty with twenty four pay cycles in a year, it works out to be forty-two thousand dollars, which is my annual salary," Mammen replied avoiding direct eye contact. The officer looked at the pay stub again which showed a two-week pay of $1750, scribbled something on the pay stub and quickly regretted striking the pay stub with the pencil a few moments ago.

"Shit, I don't have time for this," he said without looking at Mammen and pressing the rubber end of his pencil with his thumb.

"It's too cold."

The weather had indeed been miserable in Toronto in the past week, especially in the last two days. The headlines in the local newspapers had declared it to be the snowstorm of the century with temperatures dipping twenty degrees below zero Celsius. Mammen cursed his luck, convinced that had he decided to come to the US consulate in Toronto a week earlier or a week later, the snowstorm of the century would have happened then.

To Mammen it seemed like a cruel design of fate to have endured the wait in a queue from 6:20 in the morning to enter the consulate which opened at 8 o'clock - in record cold that would probably stand for another century. Now at the end of this long and torturous wait was a visa officer sitting in a heated room, tapping his pencil, who could reject Mammen's application for a visa renewal because he, the officer, didn't agree with the temperature outside the building. Today, even Amul, would have had to agree with him about the timing of the century's snowstorm, thought Mammen as he grinned nervously to himself, while the burly visa officer ruffled through his papers again. To take his mind off what the visa officer might ask him next, Mammen turned his head around and immediately caught the nervous look on Gundu Rao, seated between an old Asian woman and her son.

"Haallo, I'm Gundu Rao working for Goodyear in Ohio," was how he had introduced himself to Mammen an hour ago, when Mammen had been seated where the old Asian woman was now sitting. There was an emphasis on "Goodyear" and this did not escape Mammen. With that brief introduction Gundu Rao had made Mammen realize that although they were both here in the US consulate for the very same purpose of renewing their US visa, and they had probably come to the US as students for the same dream, Gundu Rao must have walked a very different path than Mammen since the day they arrived in the States, until today, and probably their paths would diverge again as soon as they walked out of the consulate.

The music of Boney M blared into the humid night of west Texas from a cheap used speaker on the third floor of a run down apartment building. There was a slight breeze blowing south eastwardly. In Lubbock at this time of the year, when the wind blows in this direction, it carries with it an unpleasant smell of cow dung from nearby dairies. And tonight, when the wind passed by Sundown apartments it would mix with the aroma of *masala* emanating from an apartment on the third floor, producing a smell only people who were lined along the broken concrete staircase talking above the din of Boney M could describe. Of course, that is, if you asked those who were not already drunk. And on that late July night, if you walked up the staircase at Sundown, you would probably be the only one who noticed the pungent mix of cow dung and *masala.*

Amul was a riot inside the apartment, dancing, singing, and drinking, all at the same time, while eight or nine others were dancing around him all to their own interpretation of the music of Boney M. There were many more people, mostly young Indian men standing around the eight or nine watching the show Amul was putting on. Through the window that would open up every other

4

moment as the sweaty bodies of the students dancing around him would move, Amul would get a glimpse of Anusuya standing next to Mammen. He could see the two were in light conversation. Mammen seemed to be following up every giggle of Anusuya with a manly sort of laugh, not entirely artificial. But then, had you met Mammen on your way up the stairs, he would not have noticed the smell of the breeze either.

Gundu Rao was not quite sure from Mammnen's phlegmatic look whether Mammen was paying attention or whether he had not stressed "Goodyear" sufficiently. But he decided not to risk over-emphasis. He tried a different approach.

"Where do you work, Mammen?" he asked after Mammen had introduced himself.

"Oh, in New York," replied Mammen and added, "as a software engineer."

The subtle approach seemed to have run aground no sooner than it had taken flight. Perhaps, concluded Gundu Rao, Mammen was one of those engineering students who came to do their Master's in some bi-directional state university, in some god-forsaken town, in some Southern state, and who upon graduation realized he

5

could not get a job, picked up a course or two in Information Systems or Computer Science, groped his way into getting a software job in one of those software sweat shops on the East Coast, and after toiling on developing some screens for a software application or writing some petty client side Java code for six months, decided it was time to go to India and get married. Perhaps he was planning to get married to a girl his parents would have fixed up for a six figure dowry. And perhaps this girl...

"Attention everyone, you need to have exactly one hundred dollars, American!" bellowed a white middle-aged woman as she paced up and down the waiting area in the consulate. She worked for the consulate, that Mammen could tell by the authoritative way she carried herself. Her face looked as though she had not smiled in days, just like the rest of her colleagues. Just like the burly bespectacled visa officer.

"Maybe it's a job requirement," thought Mammen as he keenly observed the woman pacing up and down.

"We cannot give any change, so your visa fee has to be exact, I mean exact, no exceptions!" she continued in the same demeanor.

"Perhaps it's the weather," thought Mammen.

"Perhaps, this girl has a BA in Home Economics, but has already started taking a computer software course like Visual Basic or Oracle in a local tutorial, with pirated software of course, so she too can come and join Mammen in the sweat shop," continued Gundu Rao's train of thoughts, after the unwelcome interruption by the woman.

"This is Amita," is how Goops, as he was called, introduced his girlfriend to Mammen outside the apartment at Sundown.

"Pleased to meeetcha!" replied Mammen, putting on his Texan accent, extending his hand to Amita.

She took his hand with genuine warmness and said, "I hear you read palms."

"You betcha!" said Mammen, keeping up with the Texan theme, drawing her and Goops' right palms toward him and looking at the area under their little finger.

"Y'know, there isn't too much light to see your palm properly," said Mammen without looking up.

There was silence for a few seconds, a tense sort of silence.

"Hey, I'm kinda drunk, and there ain't much light out here," remarked Mammen not entirely untruthfully, breaking the uncomfortable silence.

7

Amita said nothing.

"She's aw'right, you know what I'm sayin'," asked Goops, beaming ear-to-ear and feeling uncomfortable with the change in mood that had set in suddenly.

"What I'm sayin' is she ain't great or nothin', but she's awright!   Ain't nothin' but a chicken wing!" he laughed.   Amita laughed too and of course so did Mammen.

This was a relief to Mammen, who did not waste any time in turning Goops' remark to into more humor. They all laughed out loudly.   Just then Nita came and pulled the three of them to a dance that the crowd had broken into.

CHAPTER 2

A Conqueror's Privilege

It was fifteen minutes past two o'clock as Mammen raced across the campus to the Human Sciences building. He was fifteen minutes late, or so he thought, as he leaped two steps at a time up the stairway. He stopped once he reached the third floor to catch his breath, but more so to look composed. He was acutely aware of his tardiness and how it would be attributed to his Indian or eastern background by the Americans he was going to meet, though he was sure they would only *think* that and never actually say it. The thought did cross his mind that they probably had a point, but he quickly tried to squash the thought with his pride.

"There you are Mammen. Thanks for coming," greeted Dr. Sarah Shepard, the Dean of the College of Human Sciences, who had invited Mammen for the meeting she had organized on this afternoon.

"Sorry I'm late," replied Mammen shaking her hand firmly as his international student advisor had suggested three years ago when he had first come to the university. He debated whether he should make an excuse as to why he was late, but his pride had not convincingly squashed the thought he had had a little earlier.

"Oh, not a problem at all," said Dr. Shepard in a lighthearted tone. "The Moroccan and Malaysian representatives are not here yet."

The meeting was Dr. Shepard's idea of bringing together high school teachers in west Texas with international students in the hope that such a tryst would result in exposing cultural diversity to teachers born and bred in places like Muleshoe, Happy, Snyder, Floydada, and Amarillo. And this knowledge would in turn be passed on to the students in their schools. It would be interesting to find the effect this trickle down theory had on students from these high schools, especially the long-term effects. How would they see foreign people like Mammen in America's Bible belt?   Would it just remain knowledge, or would such knowledge make them more understanding of other people, or would it draw them more aloof from these 'aliens'?   At least this was the idea Dr. Shepard had for her research and the paper she hoped to publish from it. Maybe two, maybe in prestigious journals, if things went well, she reckoned.   That would also end the two-year publishing drought she had been in since becoming the Dean.

Dr. Shepard called everyone's attention in the room as soon as Karim, the Moroccan student, and Hong the Malaysian student, came in.   It was 2:35.   Karim did not seem aware that he was late; if he was he did a good job of concealing it.   Hong looked a little apologetic, but that could have been because others had come earlier than he had and not necessarily because he was late, thought Mammen. Dr. Shepard wanted groups of three, consisting of two teachers and one international student, to gather around a table and have the international student answer questions the teachers have on culture, language, and the country the international student came from.   After an hour she would ask all the international students to get together as a group and this time and have a question-answer session with all the teachers.

"Ha-ai, I'm Deborah," said one of the two young women sitting around a table that had been assigned to Mammen, introducing herself. There was a distinct west Texan twang in her voice that Mammen easily detected.

"Pleased to meet you" replied Mammen, without any of the affected Texan accent he had used at the party at Sundown a week ago.

As he had expected, the question of the Indian caste system came up once the pleasant questions were over.

"Look, it's similar to the racism issue you have here. I'm not using that as an excuse, but only trying to make you relate to the situation in India. Just as your government is against it and just as most of you Americans are against it, so are the government and people of India. But casteism is alive and breathing in India, sometimes in subtle form and sometimes in very overt form, just as racism is in the States."

Luanne, the second teacher in his group interjected.

"It's a sad chapter in our history. But our society has come a long way since then in this country. And so have race relations."

12

Deborah agreed. "Y'know it's really a lot different since the civil rights movement."

"Y'know, Dr. Martin Luther King an' all," added Deborah.

Mammen nodded in agreement.

"Yes, we too abolished casteism by law after independence from the British, in 1947, about two decades before civil rights were passed in the America," said Mammen.

"But as I said, we Indians, and I don't mean all, I mean we...as a...a nation...it's practiced. Just like even after Dr. Martin Luther King and all...you...I mean... mainstream America practices racism in an invisible way. You know it's there, although you can't feel or touch it. Of course, sometimes it not so invisible because they tell it to your face, or worse you die because of who you are. So it's the same thing in India."

The women started feeling a little uneasy with Mammen's comparisons to the American situation. America, to them, was after all a shining beacon to the rest of the world. Even the mistakes in her history: invasion, plunder, genocide, slavery, and then repentance are seen in glory, because to get America where she is today, those

13

mistakes were necessary. It was unfortunate, but a tortuous bridge in history that had to be crossed. Once the bridge was crossed the victory was complete. Once victory is complete the conqueror gets to define what victory is from thereon. The conquered are assimilated.

Conquerors sometimes repent on the cruel road they have taken to become a shining beacon. When they do, there is respect and honor bestowed on them, even by the conquered, because the conqueror, now perceived as superior, is also seen as benevolent with the memory of the cruel conquest now almost forgotten.

To hear someone from a conquered society say that their society practiced racism, or a derivative of it, such as casteism, and repented for it at the same time, made it unsettling for Deborah and Luanne. It was as if the act of repentance was a conqueror's privilege and not a privilege of the conquered.

"See," Mammen continued, "We have practiced casteism for a very long time. Much longer than modern America has been in existence. But like the white folks in America, we do a good job of denying it, saying how much we have done for the downtrodden and how much reverse discrimination exists in present day India. So between the

14

two, is it your society or my society that is more casteist? Of course my Indian friends would crucify me if they heard me say this. But they would practice it the next day forgetting they just crucified me yesterday. You see that is the Indian brand of racism."

Mammen laughed. Luanne and Deborah were quiet, but smiled politely.

"How does present day Indian society see intermarriage? Between the castes...or say if you were to marry, say an American?" asked Luanne.

Again Mammen drew comparisons. "Just like America. Well, I should say we are worse. The law protects intermarriage between the religions, castes and whatever, as long as the boy is at least 21 and the girl 18. Of course that's not how our society works though. Just like say a white marrying a black or someone non-white. Your society does not encourage it, but tolerates it at best. Some would probably consider it a step down, no? Similarly marriage between different castes or religions is not something that's encouraged, but something that is tolerated. In some parts of India it's not tolerated. The price of crossing such lines could be death."

If Mammen was conveniently trying to avoid answering the personal part of Luanne's question, he had read Luanne wrong. She insisted.

Mammen was not as eloquent in his reply as he had been in his discourse of Indian casteism. But before he could elaborate, the sound of a pen, tapping gently on an empty Coke can drew everyone's attention to the front of the room, where Dr. Shepard stood, smiling. She put the can down and reminded everyone that it was time for the second part of the discussion.

All the student representatives, from nine countries, were now seated behind two long tables put side to side. In front of them all the teachers, scattered around the room, had taken comfortable positions. There were about fifteen of them.

A woman, maybe in her late twenties, stood up almost immediately, and introduced herself as Joan McNulty.

"My question to y'all is do you find it easy to adjust to life in America, especially like…in a place like Lubbock?"

The reply was immediate too. It was Eric.

"I don't know if I speak for my colleagues here today, but personally I have found it hard, and I tend to think that it's because I am an African from Kenya. Put another way, I'm a black guy with an accent. But I have to say life on campus has been good. It was pretty easy to adjust to the classes and find my way around. People are friendly on campus and they treat you well for the most part. And I have found on campus Texans to be a very helpful people. But the hard part is when I step out of the university environment, or sometimes the class environment. You see people withdraw. They seem to try to do it subtly, but to me it's very transparent."

Many of the students who were not white were nodding in agreement.

"Even on campus, if it is for a class project or a group assignment, my American classmates are very friendly and cooperative, but they draw their boundaries quite clearly. It's hard to enter their social circle."

"Yes. Yes. Americans always say I call you...I call you...but they never call!" chipped in Ling, a Chinese student.

The uncomfortable silence that persisted when Eric was speaking was abruptly broken by Ling's remark. The room was in laughter.

"She's right," agreed Dave, a white English student in the Economics department. "Even I find it quite difficult to get an American girl to call me back."

The room was in laughter again.

But Eric quickly set the mood back.

"I have a friend from Kenya who goes to university in Mississippi. I have wanted to drive down in my car to visit her. But my African American friends tell me driving over there with my sixteen hundred dollar car is risky. Not because my car may break down. But a black man driving such a car through the south is bound to attract the attention of the cops and they may give me trouble. And from what I see on TV I really fear taking such a trip. Maybe I am overreacting. Maybe nothing will happen, but I don't want to go on a trip looking in my rear view mirror all the time. And don't tell me it's just a wrong perception or I'm stereotyping. You know it can very well happen."

This time neither Ling nor Dave provided any relief, if anybody had been expecting it.

"Eric, what you are talking about is racism in the United States. But I should say in your country too there is racism, right? Don't your people beat up on the Indians in Kenya...matter of fact do you remember sometime in the

'80s there was a coup to topple Arap Moi and the first thing you guys did was to loot and pillage Indian shops and rape Indian women."

It was Mammen who had spoken.

"By you guys, don't get me wrong, it wasn't personal," he added quickly.

Eric did not reply immediately. He looked down at the table. The uncomfortable silence returned to the room.

"I don't deny what you are saying, but what I am saying is you don't expect it in America," said Eric.

CHAPTER 3

"Mirror, Mirror on the Wall…"

The music of Dwight Yoakum filtered out of the jukebox and permeated Student Body, a popular student bar just across the university campus. Inside, Amul waded his way through the crowd with the last pitcher of beer he could buy for a penny. His regular circle of friends were sitting around a graffiti-scrawled table, eagerly waiting his return. Most eager was Goops, who had started the weekend many hours earlier than the rest of the crowd. He was able to start the weekend earlier simply because he avoided going to classes on Friday. For Goops weekends started Friday afternoon with a double shot of single malt whiskey. He was able to afford such drinks for another simple reason: his father was wealthy.

Everyone in the circle of friends was Indian or of Indian descent, except Roberto, a Brazilian, and his Argentinean girlfriend Gabriella, who was there only because Roberto was there.

Amul walked into a heated discussion that had started when he went for the penny pitchers. He set the pitchers on the table, somewhat expecting a word of appreciation. But he got none. They were all looking at Mammen.

"That's bullshit, Roberto!" said Mammen raising his voice above the din of the bar and pointing his index finger at Roberto for emphasis.

"Not every Indian woman is confined to wearing a sari or what you call the costume," protested Mammen to Roberto's accusation that while Indian women are required to wear the sari, or the churidar (the 'costume' as Roberto called it), an outfit that covered the body from ankles to the neck, Indian men could wear just about any western garb.

None of the Indian girls in Amul's circle of friends were wearing traditional Indian clothes. Anusuya, Amita, and Nita were all wearing T-shirts and shorts or short skirts, just like Gabriella and many of the young women in the bar. It seemed the right attire for the punishing weather

21

outside. But it wasn't these Indian women Roberto was using as his point of argument. It was the women in India he saw on television and the women in magazine articles, and the women he saw in the streets of India that he was talking about. And even many young newly arrived Indian women he saw on campus.

Before Mammen could begin his defense, Nita and Anusuya jumped into the argument almost at the same time, but Nita having a higher pitch in her voice prevailed. Roberto leaned back in his chair in a defensive posture.

"There are tons of women I know in India who wear clothes other than the sari or the churidar!" she exclaimed, deliberately avoiding naming the alternative attires.

"Listen, what you see in western media is not necessarily what really goes on in India. The western media just shows what it wants to most of the time. When was the last time you saw how the middle class lived in India or showed when we launched our latest low orbit satellite on American TV? All the news they show about India is when something negative happens, like an earthquake, or a flood, or some religious riots. You see that's what the western media people like to report about India, because it fits the mental mold they have created..."

"But the clothes should not be above the knees, right?" interrupted Roberto, leaning forward a bit.

"It cannot be shorts or skirts like the one you are wearing Nita, can it?" Roberto continued, now with his elbows on the table. There was no immediate response from either of the girls this time. Sensing a quick victory Roberto decided to consolidate the ground he had retaken and put the finishing touches to the debate.

"And let's leave out the omissions of the American media from this argument for now please. That can be a different argument."

Waiting for a response, he took the pitcher Amul had just put on the table and refilled his plastic cup.

"That's right Rio-man!" said Goops, laughing and slapping Roberto on the back, trying to prevent this discussion from turning into a long drawn out argument. But no one else laughed.

Mammen thought he knew where this argument was going and decided not to say anything for the moment. Amul glanced at Mammen and followed suit. Gabriella seemed disinterested in the whole argument. She borrowed

23

a cigarette lighter from Goops and lit herself a cigarette. Amita was nodding slowly, but it wasn't clear whether she was in agreement with Roberto, or if she was just trying to absorb the argument. The silence didn't last long though.

Anusuya defended Nita.

"I don't see why you think it's so important that a woman's freedom is truly achieved only if her skirt is above the knees. Isn't that so sexist of the western culture? Haven't you ever thought that there are Indian women who would like to dress modestly? Why should they dress according to the definition of women's liberty according to western culture, or the Law of Roberto, the Great Brazilian Liberator of Indian Women!" she said with more sarcasm and less humor.

Roberto was a little taken aback. The quick victory he had anticipated was not going to happen, he thought to himself. He did a quick survey across the table as though he were re-evaluating a battlefield. Mammen and Amul seemed to be holding positions—the position of silence. Anusuya and Nita looked focused and very much in the battle. Amita now seemed to be in agreement with the girls.

24

Goops walked up to the bartender. Gabriella flicked the ash off her cigarette, but appeared to be paying a little more attention to the argument.

Roberto took a sip from the plastic cup.

"How many women in India can wear the short skirt you are wearing, Anu, and walk in the streets of say, some city except maybe Bombay, without being verbally harassed? Hell, Mammen, wasn't it you who told me about this thing called eve teasing, where women are verbally and sometimes physically harassed by guys on the streets? And these are women who are wearing saris, so just imagine if you went out with what you are wearing Anu!" said Roberto taking another swig from the plastic cup.

Anusuya replied, "Look, if you are so well read on India, Roberto, you should know that in many cities across India, especially young women wear jeans and other clothes on a daily basis. Now, if you are talking of rural India, yes, it's true they wear very traditional clothes. But my point is why should they *not* be wearing clothes that they are familiar and comfortable with? Why the hell should they be in western clothes? The women in urban India may wear western clothes, or traditional clothes, because they *choose* to wear what they want. And the women in rural

25

India wear traditional because they *choose* to do so. My point again is wearing a skirt above the knee is not a measure of women's liberty in a society. If so Roberto, the women on the beaches in Rio de Janeiro are the most liberated women in the world by your yardstick!"

This time everyone joined Goops in a spontaneous round of laughter. Even Gabriella. But Anusuaya was not done.

"And maybe dear Roberto, it's because you come from Rio that you are so mistakenly thinking that there is a direct correlation between a women's skirt line and her liberation!"

Roberto leaned back on his chair. "You are trivializing my argument," he said in a soft voice, much in contrast to the excited voice Nita and Anusuya had taken in their arguments.

"It is you who brought the skirt line being above the knees into the debate, not me or Nita," retorted Anusuya in a soft voice, mimicking Roberto.

"Exactly, I'm not denying that. I will concede that urban Indian women have the freedom to wear western clothes, mostly jeans or skirts that cover a good portion of their legs. But when it comes to something above the knees, it's seen as a taboo. Of course in the upper crust circle it may be acceptable. But for an average Indian woman, I stand by my argument that she cannot simply *choose,* as you eloquently pointed out, to wear a skirt like yours Anu, or a pair of shorts like yours Nita. The same goes for the rural women who are so comfortable, as you claim, in a sari in the baking ninety five degree heat, while they are cutting grass with sickles. They too cannot simply *choose* to wear anything else. On the contrary, if an Indian male chose to wear a pair of shorts he can *choose* to do so. In fact on my last trip to India, I saw many men loading trucks who were wearing Indian clothes, but had their clothes way above their knees. Way above what I wanted to see! And that's the point I was trying to make. That people wear clothes that are based on weather and the nature of work they are doing. Indian men seem to have the freedom to do it, while most Indian women do not. It's not just because they *choose* to wear what they are wearing, but it has quite a bit to do with a culture or tradition that does not grant them the same freedom to wear what they want. In that respect, my dear Anu and Nita, while there may not be a direct correlation between a women's skirt line and her liberation, the argument can be made that there is a *rough* correlation

27

between a women's skirt line and the freedom to choose what she wants. And that, in turn, is a reflection on the amount of freedom that society as a whole enjoys. So in other words, if I was visiting from Mars, using this rough correlation theory, I could in many cases report back to HQ which country's citizens enjoy the most freedom and how much their women are liberated."

Roberto paused. But he was not finished.

"By the way Anu, if you go to the beaches in Rio, be assured that you can *choose* to wear a sari. Don't think Brazil or I are forcing you, but wouldn't you rather be wearing something above the knees while you are on the beaches of Rio?"

"Oh my Gaad…Nita it's so nice to see ya," squealed a voice behind Nita. It was Lauren. Lauren hugged Nita, making sure there was as little physical contact as possible in the hug. She then waved her right hand like a wiper on a windshield to the rest of the crowd and said.

"Hi, y'all!"

Nita quickly introduced the crowd to Lauren.

"Well, you know Mammen, Goops and Amita," she said, pointing to each one of them.

Mammen and Goops both nodded and grunted a greeting. Amita smiled and slapped Goops and Mammen on their backs for their impoliteness. Lauren waved it off with a laugh. Nita introduced the others. And then she came to Roberto.

"Lauren, this is Roberto. He has taken it upon himself to liberate Indian woman."

"Nice to meet you. Don't mind her," said Roberto.

"And where is that accent from?" asked Lauren, shaking his hand, much like a school teacher would ask a pupil on the first day of school.

"From *Brasil*," replied Roberto.

"And this is Gabriella," continued Nita.

"Hey, I'm Gaby and my accent is from Argentina," said Gabriella tersely, waving her hand like a windshield wiper, much like Lauren had done earlier.

It was easy to notice the sudden redness that had rushed onto Lauren's face. Roberto had gotten up to shake Lauren's hand when he had introduced himself and he was now standing beside Gabriella. He gently put his hand on her shoulder and gave it a squeeze. She smiled.

"Listen, great meeting y'all, but I gotta run. I'm with some of my sisters. We dropped by to get a coupla

29

shots before we head out to Jake's Barn." Jake's was a popular country western dance club that fraternity boys and sorority girls frequented.

With that Lauren left. She did not wave good-bye.

Goops was at the bar trying to attract the bartender's attention. Mammen followed to give him a hand. Nita and the other girls went to the bathroom. Roberto seemed to be relieved by the interruption. He walked to the jukebox.

"If you have had enough of it, just imagine how desperate I am!" said Amita to Nita as they walked back past the bar counter to their table. It was just as Goops and Mammen were coming back with the next round of drinks.

"I'm here now baby, I can take care of your desperation!" said Goops.

"It's not what you are thinking you clown! You don't even know what I was talking about!" replied Amita.

"Enlighten me, baby," said Goops as he set the drinks on the table, beaming ear to ear.

Gabriella and Amul made room for the glasses.

"What you guys squabbling about?" asked Amul.

"Nothing, it's just…"

"Oh, sorry if it's girl talk from the bathroom, I take my question back!" said Amul, much to the amusement of all the guys.

"You guys are impossible," laughed Amita.

"Now if you must know - I was telling Nita that I could hardly wait for fall and this summer to go away."

"Why, I like it now. I know it's a bit humid now but still I think it beats those chilly winds fall brings to Lubbock. I thought it was now more like in South America," said Amul.

"It is," agreed Amita, who was actually from Trinidad. She was three generations removed from India, her ancestral motherland.

"But it makes me go dark. And the hotter it gets the darker I get."

"And as it gets colder, the lighter you skin becomes and thus your desperation for fall right baby?" remarked Goops.

"God, how shallow can you go Amita...you want a season to change just so that your skin will look a little lighter!" exclaimed Mammen.

31

"And you don't find it shallow that Indian guys like you want fair, wheat complexioned women as their brides?" Anusuya shot back.

The adjectives Anusuya used were deliberately the same adjectives found in the matrimonial columns of Indian newspapers. People like Anusuya would use those kinds of adjectives to describe herself in such columns; if that were the way she would find her bridegroom. But she was sure she would be getting married to Amul. They had already talked about it. And she knew Amul wouldn't care whether she was wheat complexioned or not.

People like Amita and Nita were on the darker side and could not really pass themselves off as wheat complexioned. But the colder months of Lubbock helped.

"You would still look dark to me, summer, fall or winter," said Gabriella taking a sip from the cocktail Goops had brought. Gabriella was a Caucasian, of German descent - two generations removed from her ancestral fatherland.

"Don't you tan?" asked Nita pointedly.

"Yeah, sometimes. But I'm not obsessed with it."

"But why do you tan sometimes?"

Gabriella reached for her cigarette pack. She motioned to Goops for his lighter. He pushed it across the table.

"To look a little better I suppose," said Gabriella.

She lit her cigarette and blew the smoke away from the table and continued.

"But let me assure you that my marriage chances are not going to be hurt by not spending time under the bulb. See it's like for us...you want to deck up a little...yeah I'd go to the salon a few times after winter. If not, hey it's not such a big deal that I have to mention that I am tanned in the personals column. Why aren't you just happy with your natural color? How I say this...in your culture you seem to be obsessed with it. Am I right?"

None of the girls responded.

I saw Nita wave at me as I entered Student Body. I waved back to acknowledge her. It was more crowded than usual I thought. A lot smokier too. When I got to the table I was teased for arriving late from the department. I began to explain how I had got caught up with some urgent work my professor needed, but quickly regretted going down that road as I heard groans in unison.

"Ok...Ok...what do you all want for your next round?" I asked.

With the orders memorized, I stood behind the growing line around the bar. It was past 11:30. I looked out through the window. The leaves on the trees were standing still. Not even a light breeze to cool the night, I thought. I felt relieved to be inside the bar with the air conditioning.

I wished the summer would go away. I wished for fall.

CHAPTER 4

Peace, Rain, and Prosperity

The dirt road wound away from the tarred road that would take you to Roma if you went southeast from Maseru, until it forked at a painted wooden sign. The paint had worn off, but it wasn't hard to read what the sign said: SAVE THE CHILDREN HOUSE. Beneath the sign there was an arrow pointing westerly. The east side of the fork would wind down a slope until it abruptly stopped in front of an iron gate painted in metallic silver. On the other side of the gate, about twenty feet away, stood a modest red brick house, which was where I grew up.

I was trying to get to this dirt road one night walking beside the tarred road. There was no constructed sidewalk to speak of, so I just followed the beaten path. I had gone to see a friend at Queen Elizabeth II Hospital, stayed there longer than expected and lost track of time. A family friend was also there and offered to drop me home. Since I was only fifteen they were worried about letting me walk home by myself. But I insisted that I should walk. It was one of those nights when it felt good to walk. The walk would be only about twenty minutes at the most and besides it wasn't that late, I reasoned. I looked at my watch. It was only 8:30. I lit up a cigarette as soon as I got out of the hospital.

"Hey…*Likula…Likula…emela*!" someone shouted behind me as I came close to a traffic circle, which was where I would take the road to Roma. I glanced back as though to make sure the racial slur was actually directed at me. I could see a group of people standing at a bus stop, all Mosotho people, and a Mosotho man, maybe in his early twenties walking toward me. He was well dressed in a baggy sort of trousers and patent leather shoes. There was nothing to confirm. He was a *tsotsi*, an urban thug, and he was out doing his job. I debated what to do. I could make a run for it. Once I am on the dirt road he would drop his pursuit if he chased me, because he may not be familiar with that area. On the other hand the dirt road was a good

36

five minutes away and he could out run me. If he caught me things could get violent. I kept walking pretending I did not hear him.

"*Likula*...I say wait!" he said in English this time. The racial tone worried me. He may not be after my wallet or wristwatch after all. He may have changed his agenda for the night when he saw an Indian.

I walked toward a streetlight, which was dimly lit, and stopped under it.

"Are you talking to me?" I asked in Sesotho.

"Do you see any other coolies here?" he sneered in Sesotho.

I kept quiet.

"*U ya kae*?" he asked.

"Just home. I live not too far from the school over there," I replied in Sesotho.

He seemed to be taken aback.

"*He Banna!* You speak Sesotho just like a Mosotho!" he exclaimed.

"I speak it well."

"I thought you were one of those damn foreigners who just come to make money in our country and don't care about learning our culture or language."

37

"I went to school there," I said, pointing to the school by the dirt road. The school was overwhelmingly Mosotho, unlike the prep school in town, which was dominated by expatriate Europeans, Indians, Chinese and some wealthy Mosothos. It was the sort of school that included equestrian sports in its curriculum. He had probably mistaken me as a graduate of that school.

The *tsotsi's* demeanor changed completely. I felt relieved. I offered him a cigarette, which he accepted very graciously.

"I'll walk with you till you get to the dirt road," he said.

So my would-be assaulter and I walked beside the tarred road. He had started to speak in a mixture of English and Sesotho. He enquired how long I had been living in Lesotho and if I liked living here and such questions that I later always got asked by natives when I moved to other countries in Africa, America, and even India.

We continued our conversation until we came up to the school where the dirt road began from the tarred road that would take me to Roma. He stopped and shook my hand. But before I let him go, I had to know one thing from him.

"Supposing I hadn't spoken Sesotho fluently, what would have happened?"

"Working knowledge of Sesotho would have been enough. That's all I wanted to hear. I didn't expect anything more from a foreigner. I am not unreasonable."

But he hadn't answered my question. I repeated it.

He smiled wryly and winked.

"If any *tsotsi* gives you troubles in these parts in future just mention my name. They won't bother you then. Don't mention me by my real name of Mpiti, they know me as Double O around here."

"I'll remember that," I said.

He turned and left.

"*Khotso,*" I said as I waved to him.

He turned back, waved and returned the traditional greeting of peace in English.

"I heard over the radio that the Prime Minister of South Africa, John Voster, said that South Africans are not to be blamed for the recent violence in Kimberly between Mosotho and South African miners. He warned that such accusations by Lesotho would only deteriorate the relationship between the two countries."

A Close World Apart

I was reading from a prepared text I had made in the morning, listening to the local morning news, before I came to school. Everyday this ritual of reading something on current events in front of the whole school during the morning assembly was required. Today it was my turn. Since I was a foreigner I only had to read it aloud in English, but most of the school had to do it in both English and Sesotho. I always made sure the piece of news I brought to read when it was my turn was actually genuine. Only the very brave-hearted, or the ones who forgot until assembly time that it was their turn, would attempt to create news. Most often than not, one of the teachers would recognize that the news piece was fabricated and the punishment would be getting whipped in front of the assembly just before the closing song. I don't know what happened to repeat offenders because I never saw one.

Having delivered my news piece I was confidently walking back to join the line for sixth graders when Mrs. Kolobe, a sixth grade teacher whom students referred to as the 'Green Danger,' called after me. I walked to her in trepidation.

"Mrs. Kolobe, it was on the 6:30 news on Radio Lesotho," I said.

40

She smiled. "I know that. I heard it too. But, Thomas, you have forgotten your school tie."

A sudden rush of fear gripped my body as I reached to feel my throat. I had forgotten the school tie. And to be caught by Mrs. Kolobe! Why hadn't Mrs. Mutaung, or Miss Qacha, or Miss Porri caught me? I had to get caught by the Green Danger herself!

"Don't just stand there looking blank. Come stand beside me and face the assembly," she said in a more stern voice.

I didn't understand why she had asked me to face the assembly.

"Now let us all sing the Lord's song as the closing song today," said Mrs. Mohale, the school principal to the assembly.

A girl from the seventh grade, the senior most class, stepped in front of the assembly and began to lead the school in the Lord's song. Mrs. Kolobe said I should also join in the singing. But I could not. She had put her thumb and index finger on my arm and started squeezing it with all her might. I now realized why she had wanted me to face the assembly.

41

The assembly was soon over and we marched to our class. The march was led by our class monitor, but only until we turned the corner of the building behind which the assembly took place. Once the corner was turned, the monitor would be toppled from the head of the line by some conspirators, mostly in a peaceful and playful coup.

As soon as we entered class Monyane, Bataung and Mosako came by to let me know they really enjoyed the facial show I delivered with the stimulus Mrs. Kolobe had provided during assembly. I said something back in anger. They all laughed. But they dispersed quickly to their desks as Mrs. Kolobe walked in with her mathematics textbook in her hand. Something struck in my mind just then.

"Hey *muna*...have you all done her homework?" I asked.

Monyane and Bataung nodded that they had, but Mosako looked aghast.

"Okay, children have you all done my homework?" Mrs. Kolobe asked as soon as everybody had settled behind their desks.

"Yes, Mrs. Kolobe!" was the chorus.

"I don't think I heard everybody's voice in there," she said, squinting her right eye and looking to the back of the class.

"Those who didn't do it, please stand up."

Two boys and a girl slowly got up.

"Don't make me repeat what I said," said Mrs. Kolobe.

I turned my head around. I could see a thoroughly shaken Mosako getting up slowly. I gave him a smile showing my teeth. I could see Monyane and Bataung doing the same.

It was about Mosako and my other two friends from primary school, Monyane and Bataung, I was thinking of while I walked down the dirt road after the *tsotsi* and I had parted ways. I felt relieved that nothing untoward had occurred. It could have, as it wasn't uncommon, for foreigners to be roughed up by the natives every now and then. But I felt disappointed that in spite of having schooled and grown up with the natives, I was picked on and subjected to prejudice solely for looking different than them. Many years later in Lubbock, after I had traveled and lived in a few more countries, I realized how naïve I had been for feeling disappointed that night.

43

I stopped where the dirt road forked by the sign that had its paint worn off. From there I could see the lights in the living room and kitchen of the brick house where I lived. I thought for a moment and took the road to Save the Children House. I had a friend who lived at the House. I had known him since graduating from primary school and joining the school by the dirt road. I wasn't sure if the gates of the House would be closed to visitors at this time, but I felt the need to see my friend.

The gate was indeed closed when I got to the entrance of the campus of the House. The House was a project jointly funded by UNICEF and the local government to provide lodging and education for poor handicapped children who showed promise in their education. As I approached the House I heard the dogs barking, but I knew they were pretty harmless, so I slipped through the barbed wire fence and into the campus.

I found my way to room number 5-A and through the small window I could see Bafana talking to someone I did not know. I decided not to interrupt them and turned around to go. But Bafana saw me passing by the window.

"Hey, Thomas I haven't moved!" he shouted out of the window. I smiled and walked back to his room.

44

"Why are you here so late? Did the guards let you in? Or did you sneak in? Are you in trouble?" he asked all in one breath.

I sat on a stool beside his bed. I introduced myself to his friend who seemed to be struggling to light up a broken cigarette. I offered him one from my packet, but he waved it away saying he only smoked Gunston cigarettes. But Bafana did not wait for an offer. He reached out and took the whole pack. He lit one up, threw the pack on his bed and said.

"Thomas, you didn't answer me. Don't worry about Poone being here. He is OK."

I narrated to him what had happened on my way back from the hospital. He listened very attentively without interrupting me. After I had finished he said nothing for a while. Then he looked at me very gravely and asked, "If he had just robbed you and left, you would not have been so bothered, would you?"

I nodded in agreement.

"Racial slurs sting badly, when they are not said in fun, don't they?" he continued, not expecting an answer back.

"Lucky for you that you speak Sesotho like us or else my man…I think you would have gone back to the hospital and this time not to see your friend."

"That's the part I find hard to take. That he judged me solely from my appearance," I said.

"People do that to me everyday when they see me in my crutches," he said pointing to the pair of crutches sitting next his bed.

"But of course they don't do that as directly as what this *tsosti* said to you. But I know the way they behave they have already judged me. I go through this every day Thomas and I am in my own country with my own people. You see, your crutch is your appearance—your race."

I looked away from Bafana and said, "That's not the way it should be."

"Yes, my man. You will understand the world better when you grow up. If we were all cripples for just a day maybe we wouldn't be calling each other coolies or Kaffirs…then maybe we wouldn't be so apart. Then maybe there would be more people like you and me sitting in a room like this, smoking and talking like friends."

Poone had finally lit his broken Gunston cigarette. He tipped the ash into a paper cone he had made as an ashtray.

"You see, my friend, the other problem is that some of your people treat us as though we speak an inferior language that is not worth learning, or even paying attention to, because we are black and Africans...that becomes our crutch in their eyes. That's just how the Boers see us across the border in South Africa. So actually like Bafana said, you got lucky that Double O was a tsotsi who could tell the difference between the types of Indians," said Poone.

I did not know what to say. After some time Bafana spoke.

"So have you found out when you are leaving?"

"Not yet. I have to wait till my parents get back from Swaziland. But it will be in the next month or two," I said

"Where are you going?" asked Poone.

"He is going to India to continue his studies, so this could be the first and last time you see him Poone," answered Bafana.

"I hope you won't forget Lesotho and us because of Double O!" laughed Poone.

"Can you forget a country that gave you all your memories?" I replied.

"Of course you can never forget her!" said Bafana with a wink. I punched him on his shoulders. I got up to go as I was sure Mr. Rajgopal, who had moved into the brick house when my parents left, would be getting worried if I did not get home soon.

Bafana picked up his crutches and walked me outside. He was worried that I would run into one of the guards so he asked Poone to accompany me until I was out of the compound. Poone and I walked without saying much to each other so as not to attract any attention from the guards. When we got to the barbed wire fence, Poone waited until I had slipped out. I thanked him and extended my hand through the wire.

"*Khotso, Pula, Nala,*" he said as he shook my hand firmly.

CHAPTER 5

The Melting Pot

The summer finally yielded to fall. The leaves of the trees on campus were slowly turning brown and with the harsh winds blowing from the north, the trees were gradually getting denuded. But the winds brought cooler weather. The fall Amita had been longing for was finally setting in.

The campus population exploded as students returned from the summer break and new wide-eyed freshmen could be spotted from the bursar's office to the greasy pizzeria next to Student Body. Before the semester was over some of the more resourceful freshmen would find their way into Student Body.

"Read page one and then the editorial," said Anusuya as she thrust a folded copy of the *University Times*, the campus daily newspaper, into Mammen's chest.

"Why can't you just tell me?" protested Mammen.

"No, read it and tell me what you think," said Anusuya.

"I have Dr. D's class in five minutes. I'll see you for lunch at the courtyard at 12:40. Try keeping central time and not Indian stretchable time. Please!" said Anu as she hurried out of the graduate students lounge.

I was just walking out of the courtyard when I caught sight of Mammen sitting alone at a table in the courtyard. Since I was in no hurry I walked up to his table.

"Take a seat if you have time," said Mammen.

"My prof. and I submitted the paper to the journal yesterday. So I got all the time in the world," I said pulling up a chair beside him.

"Waiting on someone?" I asked.

"Yeah, Anu. She should be here any minute."

"She wanted me to read this. Why don't you read up on it too while we wait for her. You know she will insist on it if she sees you here. Of course, you still got time to make a getaway before she shows up."

I sensed he wanted me to stay. Besides, when Anu was fired up about something it was always better to have someone with you.

"I'll stay," I said, taking the paper from him.

"Now look who's keeping Indian Stretchable Time?" teased Mammen as Anu threw her backpack on the table.

"Listen, Dr. On-time-for-the-first-time, I got held up by this idiot who kept asking questions at the end of the class and I have told you how Dr. D loves to go on and on even for a simple question. Hey, besides I am only 10 minutes late!"

"Stop the squabble and get on with what you want to talk about. I don't have too much time to fritter away," I said.

"Hey who asked you to be here in the first place," retorted Anu laughing. Mammen shook his head in agreement.

"Anyway, did you also read it?" she asked looking at me.

"Skimmed through it. But Mammen here has pored over it. So why don't you start your interrogation with him, while I go over and get a bite to eat," I said getting up in order to reinforce my intention.

"Ok *yaar*, grab me a Caesar salad and a Diet Coke!" she said as though that was the price for absenteeism. Small price to pay, I thought as I asked Mammen if he needed anything.

He asked for a beer. I slapped the newspaper on his head and tossed the paper on the table. I had only walked a few paces before I could hear Anu starting her rapid fire questioning.

I got a sandwich and a soda and settled down on a table in the food court. There was a copy of *University Times* on the table that someone had left behind. I started reading the article Anu was talking about. It seemed like a petty crime to me at first. Apparently some fraternity boys had gone and stolen some construction material from a construction site in town. They had gone in the cover of darkness and helped themselves to bags of cement, timber and some reinforcement bars. It seemed as though they did it as a prank. Anyway, the total cost of the stolen materials came to around two thousand dollars. All this was out in the open now, as the Lubbock police had tracked the perpetrators after a complaint from the owner of the construction site.

It looked like a funny story to me. Typical of what you would expect of fraternity boys, or for that matter, overactive undergraduates. The police, the story continued to say, confiscated the stolen material and the owner said he would not press charges. All he wanted was an apology and a few hours of community service from the fraternity. I read the story again, because I didn't understand why Anu was so fired up over what seemed to be a stupid crime by a bunch of frat boys. Maybe it was because frat boys were involved, I thought.

I could see Anu taking this angle because the frat boys at the university were always advertising any charity work their chapters did, no matter how small. They always made a big deal out of it. And it was easy for them to do the advertisement through the campus paper, because fraternity and sorority members controlled most of the student union. And they were always trying to play down the partying, the binge drinking, and the cliques with the sororities they mostly engaged in. But still, I thought, this hypocrisy was an open secret to everyone who did not belong to a fraternity or sorority—not enough reason to fire

53

up Anu. I hurried eating what was left of my sandwich, took a few sips of the soda and walked to a receptacle to dispose the trash. My curiosity to know what stirred up Anu sped me toward their table in the courtyard. But soon I realized I had forgotten to get Anu's food. I walked back and stood in line in front of a kiosk. When my turn came I told the woman behind the counter that I needed a Caesar salad and a Diet Coke.

"You Indian?" she asked as she handed me my order.

"Yes," I said.

"Where are you from?" I asked.

For a moment she did not reply. She looked a little stunned.

"I'm from here," she said.

I pocketed the change she gave me and said thanks.

"You are welcome," she said. Her voice had lost some of the feistiness it had had when she had taken my order.

When I got to Anu's and Mammen's table they hardly noticed my presence until Anu saw the salad I had placed directly in front of her. They were arguing. She opened the plastic lid of the salad and motioned for a fork I

54

had forgotten, all the while saying something to Mammen. I walked back to the food court, grabbed a plastic fork and a few napkins and got back to the argument.

"The only question I have is how much hate mail Megan is going to get. It would have been a little enlightening if people at least wrote letters with the kind of defensive points you are making, Mammen," said Anu.

"What do you mean defensive? Why should I be defending the frat boys in the first place? I am just trying to tell you that yours and Megan's point cannot be taken for granted as truth without the event actually happening or some indication that there is a good probability of such an event happening," he replied almost as soon as she had finished.

I sat there saying nothing and finally they must have realized that I had been sitting there without understanding their argument. They looked at each other and then Anu said.

"You tell him Mammen, while I eat some of this salad."

The point Anu shared with Megan, the editor of the *University Times*, said Mammen, was that the frat boys had got away lightly because they were white, belonged to a fraternity, and wore designer khaki pants. Had this crime been committed, Megan had argued in her editorial, by some black or Hispanic kids, they would be facing jail time and, of course, a collective shrug from the overwhelming white community as though they expected no better from the black and Hispanic communities. There would have been no mercy from the owner of the construction site. No apology or community service from these kids would have sufficed.

Mammen looked at Anu as though he wanted her to continue the briefing, but Anu was busy sipping the Diet Coke. She motioned Mammen to continue.

"Well, anyway, I don't think its right for Megan or Anu to jump into such a conclusion. For one thing, this owner could just be a nice man and may have extended the same mercy irrespective of who did it. It's not like the material was taken and sold for profit to buy drugs or something. He probably understood that this was just a prank and in such a case he would not care about the race, or whether they wore nice brand name khaki pants, or cowboy boots."

"Well, did you throw in the buying drugs part consciously?" interjected Anu.

56

Mammen paused. For a moment he looked as though he were going to defend the veiled accusation that Anu had just hurled at him. But he kept quiet. Anu continued with her salad.

"Getting back to what I was saying," Mammen continued, facing me, "my question is how can Megan come out with an inflammatory editorial? I mean, why create an issue out of a non-issue unless she is doing it for publicity?"

"That's true," I said, "But using your line of logic it would have been a non-issue too had the crime been committed by blacks or Hispanics, right? Because it would have been an open and shut case, with certain individuals, who happen to be minority kids, stealing and getting caught and getting thrown in jail for it right? It would have got a few lines of print. And that would be that. A non-issue, which does not deserve being turned into an issue."

"Only problem is," I continued, "you would have assumed if the kids who did it happened to be white kids, they too would have been thrown in jail. A non-issue. End of story! Right, Mammen?"

"But since it happened to white kids the story did not end that way. They got away with it and if people like

Megan and Anu don't make an issue out of it, who will stop and think how much racism was involved and how much benevolence on the part of the owner, was involved?" asked Anu, completing her and my argument.

"And I think it's the job of people like Megan to bring out such issues for discussion. If she doesn't, she really is not doing her job," I added.

"Good job, *yaar*!" declared Anu giving me a slap on the back.

"I'll grant you this," said Mammen, "you guys are right that if some deserving issues are not poked they will remain as non-issues. But what still worries me is in the process we may, I say may, have forgotten the kindness of the construction site owner."

Anu was right on the type of mail Megan would receive. Many of them were hate mails, but she did not mention their content in the editorial she wrote the next day. She pointed out that while she had been expecting counter points to her editorial on the previous day, she was quite disappointed that most letters were of low quality with little substance and bad language. She noted, hilariously, that one of the letters mentioned, in strong language, that white liberals like her should pack their bags

58

and buy a one-way ticket to New York City. This part of the country, especially this town, the letter continued to argue, was for people with old-fashioned conservative family values. What those values were, the writer did not mention, Megan noted in her editorial.

The next day there were so many letters to the editor that the *University Times* dedicated a whole page to publishing some of them. This time a lot of them, although they did not all agree with her original editorial, were in support of Megan's right to publish what she wanted. Many of the letters also comforted her saying she was more than welcome in Lubbock and that it was the writer of the letter, suggesting she buy a one-way ticket to New York City, who should leave town.

Anu made it a point to remind Mammen and me that she was right on the reaction Megan's original editorial would create. She seemed so affected by the whole incident that she ended up writing a letter in to the editor, which the *Univeristy Times* published. But the article struck a new chord with the readers. In her article Anu said that the negative backlash against Megan's article exposed the soft underbelly of southern American tolerance to the democratic practice of freedom of speech and press. She also argued that while most southerners can talk a good deal about the land of the free and southern values, they lacked the broad mindedness or the ability to practice what they preached especially when it came to accepting a thought from someone who did not look like them. She ended her article with the question. "As a foreigner, I ask, is this what old-fashioned conservative family values are all about?"

I winced when I read that last sentence. I immediately phoned Anu, but I got only her answering machine. She returned my call at my graduate student office later that afternoon. I advised her to lie low for a few days because I feared someone might harm her. She started laughing. She sensed that I was getting annoyed, which made her laugh all the more.

Finally she said, "Look *yaar*, when I wrote that article I thought of the consequences. It's not the first time this has happened. In Delhi, at my old school, I had written something, which inflamed the feelings of some upper caste boys and they knocked me off of my scooter and I ended up in the hospital for a couple of days. I don't think it can be as bad as that. I guess I'll hear some "foreign-bitch-go-home," slurs for a couple of days and that will be that. *Relax yaar!*"

Her confidence partially assured me that she would be OK, but nevertheless I called up Amul and told him about my fears. He seemed more sympathetic to my concerns and said he would make sure Anu avoided public places like Student Body for a week or two.

Two days later, I waited for Anu in the courtyard. I had read the letters to the editor several times. Anu's article had upset many students. The same writer who wanted Megan to buy a one-way ticket to New York City was now demanding that Anu buy a one-way ticket to Calcutta. Calcutta, possibly because that was the only place he knew in India, and it would make him sound knowledgeable to many of his readers who may not even know where Calcutta was. But some of the other letters had better depth.

One reader questioned why if Anu was so uncomfortable with southerners she did not transfer to an east coast school, or for that matter, why she had even come to America. The reader acknowledged that as a white southerner she would not defend some of the things that southerners, or for that matter, even all white Americans had done in the past. But she was proud that America, the South, and Lubbock could proudly say they had constantly been challenged with ideas from people who looked different and had constantly assimilated such ideas into the greater fabric of American culture. Isn't that why so many foreigners came to this country and settled? How many other countries could make the claim of such progress, she asked in the letter. And as a finishing touch, she ended her letter with a question similar to the one with which Anu had ended her article. "Can many of the countries from which foreign students came to in Lubbock, including India, with its complex castes and sub-castes, make such a claim?"

How far, I thought, an argument stemming from the simple act of stealing some cement and reinforcement bars had come. I wondered if the frat boys who committed that simple act were thinking the same.

I looked at my watch. It was twelve fifty and there was still no sign of Anu. I walked toward the food court and stood in line at the same fast food kiosk from which I had bought the salad and Diet Coke for Anu a few days before. The same lady who had taken my order took my order again.

"How are you doing?" I asked as she was punching in my order in the register.

"Couldn't be busier. But I like it like this!" she said.

"Say, I meet so many different kids from so many countries on this campus. I was just curious the other day," she said as she handed me my order and change.

"No problem," I replied, "I was only curious too."

As I walked back to the courtyard, I was thinking of the last letter in response to Anu's article. I looked around the courtyard and saw students of every color sitting, talking and having lunch. What struck me was that I observed the same color of people around the same table. Hardly any of the tables had the mix of colors that you would expect of a melting pot. Most of them were not foreigners, but Americans, just of different color. It was as though members of one color were oblivious to the other. I stood still and looked around the many tables in the courtyard as though I was looking at paintings on a wall in an art gallery.

I walked slowly to an empty table and put the Caesar salad and the Diet Coke on the table and waited for Anu. This time I had not forgotten the plastic fork.

CHAPTER 6

"...Who's the Greatest of Them All?"

Three weeks had passed since the controversial articles by Megan and Anu were published in The *University Times*. By now the trees on campus were mostly denuded. The cold winds would sometimes pick up dust and on some days when I looked out of the window of my apartment it looked burnt orange.

It was also the beginning of the football season. Our university team had started off well in the conference, but lost 42-7 at home to a non-conference team. It was a pity, because the strong start in the season had raised hopes of finally getting into a decent Bowl game after three years. Some local TV sportscasters had even predicted that the team would break into the national top 25 in the polls.

Many fans on campus had complained that the pollsters were overlooking the talent in the team, just because the university was located in west Texas and not in Florida, or Nebraska, or the mid-west. So they hoped this year would be the year of redemption. But now with this stinging defeat, that too on home turf, it looked like we would be heading to yet another 6-5 season, I thought, as I walked out of the stadium a little before the game had ended.

I soon realized I had plenty of company once I got out of the stadium. There was a stream of people flowing out of the stadium exits. I debated whether to go to my department to complete a set of tests I was running for my research, or just to declare the whole day wasted and head back to my apartment. Not sure on what to do, I reluctantly started walking toward the university department buildings. It felt a little strange, as though I was cutting away from a herd. But looking ahead I realized I was not alone. There were a few Chinese students walking toward the buildings too.

I heard someone call out my name. I looked back, but I could not see who was calling me. But soon I saw Roberto and Goops stepping out from the stream of people and waving their hands in an exaggerated way.

"You're going the wrong way Foreigner!" shouted Roberto, laughing, as they approached me.

"Where's your team spirit, Dog?" chipped in Goops.

"Well, we lost and I thought…" I started to explain.

"With a loss like 42-7 it's no time to think, it's time to drink!" exclaimed Roberto.

With talk like that it didn't take them long to convince me to change my mind and head to the nearest watering hole, which most often meant finding our way to Student Body.

"At least we scored a touch down. They didn't shut us out," said Goops as we settled into a corner table in the Student Body. Roberto volunteered to buy the first round of drinks. He bought three bottles of Mexican beer. It had a strong bitter taste. No one seemed too inclined to talk about the football game we lost. So we sat around the table without saying much, just watching the crowd enter the bar in small groups. I thought I recognized the face of a freshman in one of the groups. He had asked me some questions the other day in the class for which I was the teaching assistant.

"Well, well, well…look who's here," said Roberto who was facing the entrance of the bar. Goops and I turned around and saw Anu and Amul walking in. They had not seen us. Goops got up and left the table trying to attract their attention.

"So what's been going on man?" I asked Roberto.

"Well, same old same old except for this multicultural thing that's going on in our classes. I guess you are lucky to be a grad student and don't have to listen to all this shit going on about the multicultural class," replied Roberto.

"I thought it would only affect the incoming freshmen and not seniors like you."

"Yeah, that's true, but that doesn't prevent every damn cowboy from expressing his opinion about it. Ask Goops what happened in the History of Jazz class we had on Friday. There was no talk of jazz and the damn TA just let the class keep on talking about how they hated this multicultural course requirement. You would think people would like to learn about other people in the world. But here they don't want anything to do with it."

"Maybe it's because it's being made mandatory that's irking the students and not with the course itself," I

67

said. I was aware of the issue through the Letters to the Editor column of the *University Times*. I had been keeping an eye on letters replying to Anu's article, although it was old news now.

Roberto was going to say something but from the expression on his face I could guess Goops had found Anu and Amul. I turned around and saw them coming toward our table. Goops had not only brought them, but also some of his favorite drink. He put four glasses of single malt without ice on the table in a triumphant manner with his usual grin. The bar was getting very crowded now, so I gave up my seat for Anu and Goops offered his for Amul, but he declined with a shrug. So Amul and I stood around the table. I hadn't seen him in a while, so it was good to see him. We started talking and I asked how his sister was doing. Priya, his younger sister, had come from Bombay a few weeks ago for the fall semester.

Amul had put in a lot of effort in convincing his parents to let Priya go abroad for her undergraduate schooling. Their worry, as with many Indian parents, was that it wasn't a good idea to send a 21-year-old girl abroad, especially to the U.S. They had insisted that if she was determined to go abroad, then she should wait until she completed college, after which she could go for graduate studies abroad. But Amul had reminded his parents that they had allowed him to come to the U.S. for his undergraduate work. Anyway, I did not exactly know at what point his parents yielded and allowed Priya to come to the America. But I doubted if it had anything to do with Amul convincing his parents about the hypocrisy of their double standards.

Goops handed Amul and me two glasses of the single malt. I took a generous sip. It tasted much better than the Mexican beer.

"She is adjusting very fast over here," said Amul.

He saw me look at him inquiringly.

"I mean, I'm happy Priya is getting into the mix of things very fast. But I'm just worried that she found friends faster than the courses she should be signing up for fall. After all, she is here to get a good education first, right?"

He didn't look like he was expecting an answer from me. I looked toward the table and I could saw Anu and Roberto had started a lively debate. Amul grinned.

"Yeah, that's her all right. The article thing has made her more argumentative. If Roberto isn't careful he'll be wearing the sari to the Rio beach today!" he said.

It was hard to tell if the article episode had changed her in any way as Amul claimed. As long as I had known Anu, I had not known her to shy away from a debate or expressing her mind. And after the Delhi incident she had told me about, I didn't doubt she had any fear of expressing her thoughts. But then again, I thought, Amul knew her better.

"I think it's more like making it mandatory that's pissed off everyone against it. I don't think they are pissed off about learning about Hispanic or African American heritage that's turned them off. Think about it man, would you like learning Aboriginal culture if the university pushed it down your throat?" asked Goops while gently shaking his glass of single malt.

"Yeah, that's what he was saying when you went looking for them," replied Roberto pointing his finger at me.

It seemed as though Roberto was going to continue, but Anu cut in.

"To answer your question, Goops, I would love to learn about Aboriginal culture if I was living in a country with Aborigines, say like Australia...and the university wouldn't have to push it down my throat. I would take it whether it was a course requirement or not."

"Yeah, I don't mind learning about another culture —that's what I was telling Thomas before you came. And its just one course and what's the big deal...but I don't see the connection in being forced to learn about Aborigine culture just because there are Aborigines where I live, like you are saying Anu. I mean what if I don't want to learn about it. Is that not a free choice in a democratic society? That does not make me racially insensitive, so spare me that," said Roberto.

"You mean racist, don't you?" grinned Goops

I looked at Amul, and he smiled, shaking his head. The bar was getting noisier as the crowd was slowly getting drunk. Occasionally I could hear someone screaming for the head coach of the football team to be fired. This would be followed by a round of approval in the bar with plastic cups and glasses raised as if to toast the head coach getting fired. I raised my glass with the latest call to get him fired, and I realized my glass was empty. Since we were the only ones standing around our table, I asked Amul to help me in getting the next round of drinks. We jostled our way to the counter and not surprisingly there was a line. We stood in

71

the line and I saw the same freshman I had recognized earlier as my student, walking away from the counter with two pitchers of beer with the froth bleeding from the sides. He saw me and smiled sheepishly.

"See what the damn football team drives you to do," he remarked in mock seriousness.

I looked above his shoulder to the entrance of the bar. There was a bouncer checking for IDs as the students came in. The freshman turned his head around to where I was looking. I suddenly remembered the freshman's name.

"Take care, Josh," I said looking at him seriously.

Josh nudged me with his elbow and winked.

"I'll be awright," he said, and walked away.

"Don't tell me learning cultural diversity is crucial to the new global market and that kind of thing," Roberto seemed to be shouting as Amul and I safely navigated back to our table without spilling any of the drinks.

"To be honest, I am getting a little worried about Priya," said Amul after we had set the drinks down and resumed our previous standing positions.

"I thought you wanted her to explore the liberties offered in America," I said.

"Don't misunderstand me, I really do, and you know how I had to argue with my parents that the world is changing from the one they were born into. But she is coming in late from parties with her friends…and I'm just worried. The worst thing is when I try to discuss it with her she comes up with all this argument how she is 21, and can take care of herself, and this is not India."

"What you mean is you want her here in America, but conforming to Indian societal rules for an Indian girl," I said.

Amul looked irritated, but did not say anything immediately. He seemed to be allowing his anger to pass. He reached for the new pitcher of beer we had bought and filled his plastic cup, which was already nearly full.

"The average student graduating out of university in America does not need to know much about other cultures unless they are going to be working with international companies. If you think of it reasonably, most of the students graduating will not be in such positions. Let me tell you this…you know as well as I do that the corporate culture is based on white American culture for the simple reason that whites constitute, I think, more than like 75% of the population. So where is this case of the *need* to take multicultural studies? It's just a hoax the liberals are throwing in to force diversity studies in college campuses," said Roberto half shouting.

I was surprised Roberto was raising his voice as he usually argued in a slow sure-footed tone, often encouraging his opponent to loose their composure and raise *their* voices. And then he would capitalize when they would most often, inevitably slip. Maybe he wasn't fully convinced with his own argument and he was slipping, I thought. Or maybe he was trying to be heard above the din, which was growing as the crowd was getting drunk.

Someone, standing on a nearby table with a half full pitcher in his hand called for the quarterback to be fired.

"It's not his arm, it's not his arm!" he shouted.

The crowd immediately broke into howls of laughter. For a moment, so did Roberto, Anu, and everybody around our table.

"But without understanding how other cultures operate, how will you learn to communicate in a meaningful way with the rest of the world, especially if you are a superpower like America? And the 75% you quote Roberto, is declining as the minority population is increasing...so it only makes sense for Americans to start

74

understanding other cultures in the world, including the ones in their own land that are not white," said Anu swinging the mood back to the debate.

"Yeah, its pathetic the average American knows so little of the world. You know, the average Joe Shmoe won't be able to locate where England or Brazil is, if you give him an unlabelled map!" chimed in Goops. Anu was shaking her head in agreement and amusement.

"And why does the average American Joe need to know where Rio or London is on a map?" shot back Roberto. He held out both his palms at Anu as if to hold her back before he had finished.

"Hang on before you say something...I need a smoke," he said looking at me. I reached to my pocket to get him one, but Goops had already pushed his packet toward Roberto with the lighter riding on top of the cigarette box.

"Can you locate where Paraguay is or where Zimbabwe is if I gave you an unlabelled map?" asked Roberto as soon as he exhaled the first drag from his cigarette.

He did not need to put out his palms this time.

"It's not your sister, and so you can afford to use lofty arguments," said Amul.

"You are personalizing it," I replied

"Of course, it is personal to me, she is *my* sister!"

"That cannot change the truth, can it?"

"So what would you suggest? Let her go wreck herself?" Amul retorted without bothering to suppress his anger this time.

"Isn't that the same argument your parents were using to suppress her freedom in India and what you argued against?" I shot back without masking my anger either.

"So you see my point is," Roberto was saying, "people in different countries take interest in knowing about other countries that are more developed than theirs. And by developed let's be clear, I mean technologically more advanced...so don't give me any grief on what I mean by developed. That is why the average Indian and Brazilian knows about the U.S, England, and Japan, but knows little about Albania and Zimbabwe. So if you extend this theory of mine, guess who is at the top of the heap...who's the greatest of them all? So you see why the average Joe Shmoe in America can afford *not* to know about any other country, until someone else gets on top of the heap. I am not saying it's a great thing, but only that it's a natural phenomenon that can be observed in pretty much with every country and it's not something unique to the people of the United States. It's the same as why people want to know more about people ahead of them in a class ...not who's behind them."

"There is only one flaw in your afford-to-be-ignorant theory," interjected Anu taking a sip of beer from her plastic cup.

"What's that?" asked Roberto.

"Well, if citizens can afford to be ignorant of foreign affairs because they, or rather I should say their country, is higher on the heap, then who watches what the politicians and the government of the country does in terms of foreign policy? Or to put it simply, how does the citizen know what his or her government is doing in other countries. Think of it this way, Roberto, people know domestic issues and that is why politicians are careful about what they do locally, because come election time they need to come and beg for votes. They know they are being watched and therefore being held accountable. But, if they know they are not being watched in foreign policy, there's a good chance they will not be so scrupulous. So in order for the country to set good foreign policy, one that is consistent with the conscience of its citizens, the citizens should know what's going on in other countries and what their own country is doing in these countries. For the average American Joe Shmoe you mentioned, knowing to locate where England or Brazil or even Zimbabwe on a map would be a good start."

Roberto leaned back against his chair and ran his fingers through his hair.

"You got a point there," he said.

"Here, now you can wear this sari to your beach in Rio," laughed Anu making a gesture as though she was undressing herself out of a sari.

Later, as we all left the bar, Anu walked next to me and tugged me on my arm.

"Was it about Priya you guys were discussing in there?"

I nodded looking down.

"It's really bothering him. I think you should talk to him."

"I tried and we don't seem to agree."

"Not like that over there, she is not like what you think," said Anu.

We reached Anu's apartment complex gate. She hugged Amul putting her cheeks against his, said goodbye to the rest of us and ran up the stairs to her apartment. Goops and I walked toward our apartment complex while Amul and Roberto went the other way. The winds had picked up and I could feel the cold on my cheeks.

CHAPTER 7

The Department

I stood by the administrative assistant's desk, in the main lobby of the Department, waiting for her to end her conversation. From what she was saying over the phone and the giggling that followed, it seemed like a casual phone call. But, I had a feeling she was going to take her time, so I walked over to the seating area a few feet away from her desk. I sat down and picked up one of the many trade journals that were neatly arranged on a glass table. I flipped through the latest issue of one of the journals. I could not bring myself to read any of the articles. I glanced toward the assistant's desk. But she was, or was pretending, to be oblivious to my presence.

I looked at the clock on the wall in front of me. It was 9:20. I looked outside through the blinds on the windows. The apple tree in front of the Department was completely bare. Two students were standing next to it, with their hands in the pockets of their heavy winter jackets. The guy was talking and the girl standing next to him didn't seem to be listening to him.

I picked up the journal again, but my mind wandered. I started thinking of Anu.

Growing up in New Delhi, in a close-knit upper caste Hindu middle class family, she defied conventional wisdom of what she should have grown up to be. At least to me it appeared so. Delhi would have afforded girls like her sufficient freedom, maybe even more than many societies in the world. Delhi would have given her the freedom to pursue almost anything she wanted and acceptance by the Indian society at large by virtue of her being an upper caste Hindu. Few doors would not have opened to her. Of course there would have been barriers here and there being a woman, I counter argued with myself. Still, with her socio-economic background, it was hard to understand why she questioned and rebelled against what was around her. It was like being a white

81

middle class Protestant girl in America rebelling against her environment.

At what point did she start questioning whether the *sufficient* freedom given to her by the Delhi society and India were not sufficient for a woman like her? What had made her write that article on behalf of the underprivileged castes in college, that so inflamed her fellow upper caste male college mates, that made them run her off the road hospitalizing her for two months? Why did she question and rebel when she did not have to?

I looked toward the administrative assistant's desk. She was still on the phone, with one hand holding the receiver and with the other she was making a circling motion in the air with a pen, as though she were explaining something. I noticed a student, wearing a cowboy hat, standing in front of her desk, just where I had been standing some time ago. The assistant cupped the mouthpiece of the phone and asked the student to wait in the seating area. She then thanked the student with a smile.

I could feel the anger rising in me. Just less than a year more to go, I thought, that I had to put up with such petty indignities at the Department. But I suppressed my anger by looking away from her and looked out of the window through the blinds again. The two people beside the apple tree were still standing there next to each other. Then I saw the guy take his hand from the pocket of his heavy winter jacket, place it under the chin of the girl and kiss her on her lips.

I wondered if it was a single event in her life or a gradual change in thought that had made Anu question the society she grew up in. Of course that single event couldn't have been the incident that hospitalized her, because the article she wrote *caused* the retaliation from the upper caste Hindu boys. Did she come to America thinking she could find the freedom that India could not give her - only to find that neither could America? Did she find that the freedoms society offered women in America were, like in India, male defined? The boundaries are elastic, they have always been, but it was up to the woman to push the boundaries outward, otherwise the boundaries would remain static. The men would leave the boundaries as they are. When a Susan B. Anthony pushed the boundary during the suffrage movement the boundaries yielded outward, allowing American women to vote, some 150 years after American males had declared on paper that all men are created equal, without the fine print that it only applied to white land owning men. It was as if even their white wives did not count enough to be mentioned as a caveat in the fine print to their declaration.

"Hi, Tom!" said a voice behind me. I felt a hand on my shoulder. I turned around. It was Jo Ann, the administrative assistant's manager. I had known Jo Ann since the first day of my doctoral program at the Department. From that day on she had always appeared to want to help me more than I really needed. I always thought it was because I was a foreigner and she considered me a guest in west Texas, which was home to her. I felt guilty rationalizing her good-nature this way, and so I could never bring myself to ask her if it was true.

We exchanged the usual pleasantries and I told her why I was at the Department office, showing her the papers in a manila folder I was carrying. She took the folder from me and told me that she would review and sign them before the end of day.

"You can come over any time after 2'o clock. I'll just leave them on my desk, so you can pick it up, even if I'm not at my desk."

I noticed the administrative assistant was observing us. She had ended her phone conversation somewhat abruptly a little earlier.

Jo Ann walked away to her office and I turned to go. The administrative assistant smiled at me. Her demeanor toward me had suddenly changed. She even apologized for the wait I had to make. I nodded in acknowledgement, but did not say anything.

I glanced at the clock on the wall as I walked out. It was a little after 9:55. I had just a few minutes to make it to the undergraduate class I was covering for my professor.

The familiar sounds from Room 412 greeted me as I entered the classroom on the fourth floor of the Department. It looked more like a presentation room than a classroom, with stadium-like seating arching around a stage. The students seemed to be in a good mood and a little surprised to see me. Apparently my professor hadn't told them that I would be covering for him. I wasn't surprised to learn that, since my professor would often make this decision at the eleventh hour depending on whether he had a hangover or not when he woke up that morning. I didn't know for sure if this was true, but I had been in the Department for a while. Anyway, the students didn't mind me coming because as one of them had put it, I was more entertaining in teaching a dry subject than my professor was.

"Soils have a memory," I began my lecture, looking from side to side of the lecture hall trying to determine whether I had caught everyone's partial attention at least. Toward the back of the hall I noticed Stacy with a lipstick in her hand, but she was looking at me as though I had called her name.

"Yeah, that's right," I continued, "Soils remember things, just like you and me. They don't forget things that happened to them."

I saw plenty of bemused faces in front of me. I felt encouraged. It was always the first five minutes of the lecture that I found difficult to set a tone for the rest of the 45 minutes.

"They don't forget a thing...just like Stacy over there who won't forget to put that lipstick on, even though this is a soil mechanics lecture! Go on Stacy put it on... don't just sit there holding the stick!"

The class broke into laughter and some guys sitting in the rear of the room started to whistle. Embarrassed, Stacy put the lid on the lipstick and tucked it away quickly.

But then, still red in the face, she got up and bowed in an exaggerated manner, as an actor would do after the curtains fell.

I rushed down the staircase to the second floor after the lecture, walked across to the other end of the building and opened the door of the graduate student's office of the department. As I opened the door I could hear an angry voice. It was Prashant who was complaining to Lee and Aung about something to do with the money he was making as a research assistant. Apparently he wasn't happy.

"What do you think?" Lee asked me as soon as they saw me.

"I think I have just about ten minutes before Dr. Raman's class and I need to go down and have a smoke before I do that," I said without stopping, fearing I was going to be drawn into an argument.

I put down the homework the students had submitted on my desk and grabbed my cigarette box and the three ring binder I used for Dr. Raman's class. As I turned to leave I saw a note on my desk. It was from Anu, asking me to call her at the graduate student office in her department. There was only one phone for all the graduate

87

students in my office and that was where Prashant happened to be holding his public grievance hearing. But I decided to risk it and went straight to the phone without making eye contact with Prashant, or his audience. The student who picked up the phone at Anu's office informed me that Anu had just left for a class. I hung up and as soon as I turned around from the phone, Prashant held me by my arm.

"Look, if you don't have time to listen at least tell me you have written the assignment program for Dr. Snell's class," he pretended to plead.

"It's on my local drive. You know where to find it. But at least change the heading and change the variable names after you copy it," I said pulling my arm away.

A cold blast of wind greeted me as I stepped out of the Department. Lighting my cigarette I looked around the campus in front of me. All signs of late fall were visible. Black and gray coats, people walking a little faster going from building to building, and fewer people stopping and talking to each other. But the ubiquitous 8-gallon hats could be seen every now and then, no matter what the season.

I wondered if it were harder for Anu, being a woman, to express her beliefs than it would have been if she had been a man. Going against the current is hard and it must be harder if you are a woman I thought. But did that mean a woman needed more courage than a man to swim against the same current? I was thinking more of the mundane currents that we all swim against because of what we believe, not just the issues that affected women. When Anu wrote that controversial letter to the editor about the frat boys, was it harder for her because of her gender? When she argued with Roberto at Student Body about the rights of Indian woman, or the time she argued for the importance of a well-read citizenry, was it harder for her than it would have been for me, even if I said the very same things she had said?

I looked at my wristwatch. There wasn't much time to make it to Dr. Raman's class. I stumped my cigarette out and hurried toward the elevator.

"See a lot of these American students here don't want to do any of the heavy mathematics that is required in engineering. They just want to get through as though this Department is handing out liberal arts degrees! And I tell you, some of these professors are actually to blame because they sugar coat some of these courses and cut out as much heavy mathematics from the course work as possible," said Dr. Raman as I followed him into his office after his lecture. He was explaining himself why he had dismissed Laura, one of the only two American students in his class, with a joke when she had asked a rather embarrassing question about the mathematical proof Dr. Raman had written on the white board. I had come to pick up a textbook from him.

He dropped the books he used for his lecture on his desk. I felt he had more to say, what he really wanted to stay. So I remained silent.

"Some of these professors, the American ones, have actually come up to me and said the mathematical analyses I insist on in my courses are really not necessary."

He paused and laughed, shaking his head in mock disbelief.

"I think these guys don't really know the math themselves and are intimidated by it, so how do you expect them to teach the students the math they don't know?" he continued.

Dr. Raman got up from the reclining chair and leaned a little toward me from the other side of the table, his left eye squinting a little. He pointed an index finger at me.

"Do you know why these American students don't understand the math?" he asked.

I didn't think he was expecting me to answer. He did not wait for an answer either.

"Many of them do not have the foundation which was supposed to be laid in high school, but a lot of the high schools here are a joke if you compare them to the system we go through in India. So they come to college without the proper foundation and of course they are not in shape to tackle college math. And when they can't cope they just complain that they can't understand the accent of their foreign TA or professor!"

Dr. Raman was laughing. He sat back in his leaning chair and then his demeanor turned serious.

"But despite this, there are some brilliant American students that come into the Department once in a while. It would be such a pleasure having them as my graduate students...but...you see...they want American professors, read that as white, as their mentor."

He put out his hand as though I was going to protest.

91

"I have been in this town since the early '60's, you know, so it's not some imagined thing I am making up. That's the way it is here."

"But it was in the early '60's they hired you here as faculty...so..." I said, deliberately not completing the sentence.

He struck the palm of his left hand with his fist standing up from his reclining chair.

"Ha! That's true! You are right!" he said as though he had anticipated what I had just said.

He sat down and looked serious again.

"That's the other thing you will realize once you have been in this country long enough. They are quite an open and tolerant people—up to a point. They like to see you do well and be successful. But the point of tolerance goes only as far as you are not more successful than them, or equally as successful as them. You see, they don't like being eclipsed by dark-skinned immigrants. And when that eclipse happens they try to bring you down. Others, who don't have the competence to make an attempt at that, just go flat out and write racial slurs on your picket fence."

Dr. Raman looked a little dejected. His shoulders drooped a little. I avoided looking directly at him. There was silence in the room. I looked through the large windows behind him.

It was late afternoon when I finished grading the assignments the students had handed me in the morning from the soil mechanics class. I looked at my wristwatch and it was 4:47. I suddenly remembered I had to get the papers back from Jo Ann. I hurried down the stairs to the Department office. When I got to Jo Ann's office, she was not at her desk. I looked for my manila folder on her desk. It was there just as she had promised. I opened it and looked to see whether the travel budget had been approved. The signatures were there. I walked out of her office and looked around to thank her.

"You lookin' for Jo?" asked the administrative assistant with a smile.

"No," I said.

I walked back to my office wondering what I should do for the rest of the day. There was no one else in the office except for me. I saw a copy of the day's *University Times* on Prashant's desk. I sat on top of his desk and started reading the paper. There was an announcement on Page 3 that there would be a 'Take Back the Night' march on campus that evening. It was a march organized by a campus women's organization. It was meant to be an awareness event for the public to learn more about the abuses that were inflicted on women in America. It aroused my curiosity. I thought I should go and witness it.

I put on my heavy winter jacket and walked out of the Department. It was getting dark and colder. But it was a clear night. I walked toward the courtyard from where the march was supposed to begin according to the announcement in the paper.

By the time I reached the courtyard there was already a large group of people, mostly women. Everyone appeared to be holding a candle or two. One of the women was making a speech. I couldn't hear her clearly as she was not using a microphone. But she mentioned a statistic that astounded me—every nine seconds a woman is physically assaulted by her husband, or her boyfriend, or by a stranger in America. It sounded incredible and I made a mental note to verify the statistic.

I stood by the side of the road adjacent to the courtyard observing the march. These young women are in their little way making an attempt to stretch the boundaries I thought. I wondered if it was harder for the women to organize this march because it was a woman's issue than it would have been for them to organize a march for a gender-neutral issue.

I heard someone call out my name from the march. It was Anu and she was waving to me as though she wanted me to join her in the march. I slipped into the march and got next to her.

"I tried to call you back at your Department but seems you had left for a class," I said.

"I know," she replied.

"I had called you to let you know of this march," she said.

She lit me a candle and put it into my hands. She looked at me and through the glow of the candle. I could see her face was bright. She put her hand on my hand and squeezed it.

CHAPTER 8

A Conqueror's Privilege (Part II)

"It's an assault on your senses," said Dr. Shepard. She was describing her recent trip to India to a group of foreign students and west Texas high school teachers who were standing around her drinking punch. This was a follow up meeting to the one she had arranged earlier during the spring semester. She had invited the same people back, as well as some new students who had arrived in the fall semester to get feedback, especially from the high school teachers, on how their perception and the perception of their west Texas high school students had changed toward international cultures.

This meeting was more informal than the first one. It wasn't held at the Human Sciences Building, but at the

International Center's lounge, where snacks and punch were served. It was also held early in the evening so that the international students did not feel the pressure to hurry back for a class.

"But did you like your stay in India?" enquired Mammen who had just arrived, about fifteen minutes late, and joined the audience around Dr. Shepard.

"Oh, hi there Mammen, I didn't see you. Thanks for coming. Glad you could make it!" said Dr. Shepard in a slightly animated manner.

Mammen returned the pleasantries. Ivana, a student from Russia who hadn't been at the spring meeting, enquired what Dr. Shepard meant about her trip to India.

"Oh, you feel all your five senses come alive at the same time. The stimuli are constantly attacking all your senses the moment you step into an Indian city," said Dr. Shepard.

Mammen slipped out of the group and went to the table where the snacks and punch were set up. He poured himself a cup of punch. He surveyed the lounge as though he was looking for someone. He recognized many familiar faces. He could see that Hong, the Malaysian student who had arrived very late at their spring meeting, had made it earlier this time around. Hong seemed to be a lot more at ease, sitting in a relaxed position, with one hand in the pocket of his pants and the other holding a cup of punch, bantering with an attractive girl. Mammen didn't recognize her. Could be a new fall arrival he thought. After seeing Hong he reflexively looked for Karim, the Moroccan student, who had been as late as Hong at the previous meeting. But scanning the small crowd, Mammen could not find Karim. Mammen looked at his wristwatch—it was getting close to 6:45. Could Karim be later than 45 minutes? But you never know with Moroccans, they could even be as late as three hours, Mammen chuckled to himself with that thought.

Just then the door opened. It was Eric, the Kenyan student, who had said in the last meeting that he had wanted to drive to Mississippi in his student car to see his friend, but fearing racist policemen in the south never found the courage to make the trip.

Working his way with his eyes, Mammen next came to Ling, the Chinese student whose complaint in the last meeting was that she could not find an American friend.

"Why does she need an American friend?" thought Mammen contemptuously.

Obviously none of the Americans who had met her wanted to become her friend, otherwise they would have called her, and not just promised to call her. What was her fascination with having an American friend? Was it so that she would feel she was accepted in America? Or was it so that she could say she had an American friend, like saying she has an American car. Ha, an American friend is probably like having...

It was Ling's eyes, squarely on him, that interrupted Mammen's train of thought. An immediate pang of guilt and fear went through him. For an eternal second it looked as though she had read his thoughts. That's silly he assured himself. Breathing easier, he smiled at her raising his punch cup. And as though to discourage her from coming to make a conversation, he slowly turned away to the punch and snacks and refilled his cup.

The spatula in the punch bowl was missing.

"You might need this," said a voice next to him.

It was Dave, the English student, whose comments had broken some of the tension in the room during the spring meeting.

"I've hardly seen you this semester. Where have you been hiding?" asked Mammen.

"Fifteen graduate level credits, and Reena, mate," replied Dave.

Mammen laughed. He had briefly met Reena, an Indian girl who had grown up in Bahrain, at an Indian social function. She usually kept to herself and did not mingle with the other Indian students very much. Mammen remembered the amusing comment Dave had made at the spring meeting that he was not surprised that Ling could not find an American friend because he, in spite of being English, found it hard to break into American social circles. Was the lack of acceptance by the Americans the reason he had taken to the Indian crowd and found an Indian girlfriend, or was it his familiarity with Indian culture, having lived in London, that had driven him to seek friendship with the Indian students, wondered Mammen.

"You getting out this semester aren't you?" asked Mammen making conversation.

"Everyone, can we all get together around this table? I think everyone is here...and Mammen and Dave, could you two please bring over the punch and snacks."

It was Dr. Shepard signaling that it was time to get the meeting started.

"That was my plan. But it looks like I might be here one more semester," said Dave as he lifted the punch bowl.

The students and the high school teachers sat around a coffee table. As there weren't enough chairs for everyone some settled down on the carpet and beanbags. The air in the room felt a lot lighter than in the spring meeting. There was more laughter and banter too.

Dr. Shepard allowed just enough time for everyone to settle down and then in a subtly determined manner steered the meeting towards what she wanted to get accomplished.

"Well, it definitely has been an educational experience for me and I'm sure I speak for the rest of the teachers here," Luanne started. Dr. Shepard wanted the teachers' view on whether the spring meeting with the international students had influenced them on how they taught their west Texan students about international diversity.

Luanne politely looked around at the other teachers to see if any one wanted to chime in. It seemed they wanted her to continue.

"But one thing I was surprised to find was international students seemed to have so many different opinions that I don't think I can tell my students that the international view on a certain issue is this or that...I mean we can't think that here is the American view and there is the international view. I think sometimes we all just forget that the rest of the world is not one big chunk of land, but as diverse as America is, if not more."

"I agree with Luanne," said Charles, a high school teacher out of Levelland.

"However, I'm not quite sure how to pass this on to students without them actually getting to acquaint themselves with international students. Sure, I could talk to them about these things in class...but let's not forget these are high school students we are talking about and not university students, or graduate students, like we have in this room," continued Charles.

"Oh Charles, I don't think it would have made a difference, even if they were graduate students like we have in this room. And believe me I am not saying it's because they are west Texas high school students..." said Mammen without waiting to see if Charles had finished.

Dr. Shepard looked a little irritated with Mammen cutting into the teachers' time, but she was also intrigued by Mammen's statement. So before waiting to find out how Charles or someone else might react to the statement, she decided to steer the flow of the discussion.

"I'm not sure we are all on the same page with you Mammen, are we class?" asked Dr. Shepard, raising her eyebrows in an exaggerated manner and looking around the room.

"Mammen always say something strange," said Ling with a laugh. This drew some laughter from the room, including Mammen.

"Well, what I mean is that even some of us graduate international students who are exposed to international students don't understand, or should I say put their blinders on and open up only to the part of internationalism they want," said Mammen looking away from Ling.

"I have to say I'm still not completely with you," said Charles haltingly, looking around the room to see if others needed a clarification. Dave was not one of them.

"It's not so much the exposure or your age, but how open your mind is. I think that's what Mammen is saying," said Dave. And as if to reward himself for his effort in explaining Mammen, he poured himself another cup of punch.

"Look, let's take the example of what Ling had said in our spring meeting," continued Mammen.

"If I recall correctly she had said she was disappointed in not being able to have an American friend. While I sort of understand her disappointment, my point is why has she not made an effort to make friends with other international students?"

"Well, I am in America and I want to understand American culture better," retorted Ling, sitting up on the beanbag.

"I think Ling is right. I am wondering if you have made any American friends after being on this campus for four years Mammen?" asked Eric, the Kenyan student who Mammen had argued with at the spring meeting.

"Look, don't misunderstand me—it's not like I wouldn't like to have an American friend, but I am not willing to act totally American just so that I have some American buddies. I think that's ridiculous."

"I don't think anyone is asking you to be something you are not, Mammen," said Luanne entering the fray.

"Yeah, I think you have misunderstood Americans," joined Ivana, the Russian student who was eagerly listening to Dr. Shepard talk about her trip to India before the meeting had begun.

"Well, let me put it this way," said Mammen, suddenly feeling that his back was against the wall.

"I have no problems in going half the way to make a friend of another nationality. By this I mean I am willing to learn their culture and behave accordingly, but I expect that person, American or Chinese or whatever, to make an effort to understand my culture and behave a little like an Indian, just as I learn to behave a little American or Chinese. So he or she has to meet me half way. I am not interested in making an American friend at the expense of total assimilation. And as Eric said, it's true I have been here for four years, and to answer his question the answer is no. I have American acquaintances, but no I do not have an American friend."

"But you in their country. You should be making the bigger effort if you want to learn American culture," said Ling as though it was an obvious fact.

"Oh, I understand American culture. You can learn it through reading, from television, and the acquaintances I told you about. But what I have noticed from my years here is that you will be accepted into an American social circle and that may lead to some friendships, if you show that you are sufficiently Americanized. It's like they are saying, "here's the bar and if you want in you have to clear this bar," as though it is some sort of exclusive privilege that is being granted for assimilation. And you know something else..."

"But..." began Ling. But Mammen raised his voice quickly and she withdrew.

"Let me finish Ling. Yeah, the something else I was talking about is international students behaving as though they have actually got into an exclusive club by virtue of clearing this bar. I mean, I know even among most Indian students, there is some sort of implicit pride in mentioning your American friends - that is white Americans mind you. I think it is this same eagerness to belong to this kind of club, to show to her fellow Chinese friends that she has been bestowed with this privilege by Americans...and ...you see how ridiculous this sounds? But sadly I think it is a truth that no one speaks about, but everyone knows."

Mammen paused as though to deliberately allow Ling or anyone else to refute what he had just said. But no one did.

"When you actually say it is some form of privilege to be accepted into this friendship circle, you are holding the people who are giving you this privilege on a pedestal and if you hold them on a pedestal, consciously or unconsciously, you are giving them right to set the bar. But these very same people, like the Indians I was talking about, are quick to complain when they perceive discrimination from Americans."

"But how about discrimination within your own society? You seem to be quick at jumping on other cultures. Last time we met it was about the Kenyans, this time it's about the Americans and the Chinese. To be fair, don't you think you should dish out something on your society's unique form of setting the bar and a section of your society having these privileges you were talking about," said Eric heatedly.

"By the way, don't take this personally, but please tell us about the Indian caste system." With that Eric moved closer to the table in the middle where the punch and chips were kept.

107

Mammen hesitated for a moment. Eric did not.

"I come from a village near Mombasa, but for my university I went to Nairobi and that is the first time I came in close contact with the Indian community in Kenya. Before I came to Nairobi, I just knew that Indians are people who mostly kept to themselves in Kenya. I never thought too much about it until I came to Nairobi. That's when I met Indian students on campus. Now these Indian students were born and bred in Kenya. So I guess you could call them Kenyans. So I came across these students on campus and became friends. I must admit it was not very difficult to make friends with them. I would even describe them as warm, and not aloof like the American students I saw on campus here," said Eric in a slow and relaxed manner.

"But as I got closer to them, and especially close to an Indian girl, I realized there was an invisible bar, which no matter what, they would not let me cross. Because, I was Kenyan, an African. No matter how Indianized I became, or as Mammen said earlier, total assimilation, the Indians would not accept me, even if I cleared the bar they set. That is how ingrained their caste mentality is—it is in their fiber. She said she had no problems with me being Kenyan, but that her parents and community would not take it well at all…and since she didn't want to hurt her parents…"

Eric looked down into his almost empty cup of punch, said nothing for a moment, then looked up, looked squarely at Mammen and spoke.

"It was the hurt that came out of this experience of mine that I started understanding what the caste system is all about."

Eric looked pained as he was talking. He looked away from Mammen.

"And later in my years at the university I came to understand it wasn't just to African's that they do this. They do it to themselves. They classify people based on their birth. The irony was not lost on me. Here I was trying to clear the bar by Indianizing myself, not realizing at that time that some Indians themselves would not clear the bar because of their caste. And who sets the bar? Is it the upper caste ones who set this bar or the lower caste ones who give the upper caste the privilege to set the bar?"

Eric paused. He raised his cup and finished the punch that was left in it.

"And what happened to that Indian girlfriend you made?" asked Ling.

"Well, I kept in touch with her, as she wanted to remain friends, and the rest of the Indian friends I made, for a while…but after sometime I realized I wasn't being honest with myself and I broke it all off."

Two hours later the meeting wound down. Mammen walked out of the International Center with Eric arguing about the university football team's chances at avoiding another embarrassing loss in the coming home game that weekend. On their way out they met Dr. Shepard, who was seeing some of the teachers to the door.

"Dr. Shepard, did you like your stay in India?" asked Mammen for the second time that night. This time he got a reply.

"It was," she said, "interesting."

CHAPTER 9

The Picnic

I looked outside through the window of the living room of my apartment. It looked like a clear spring day in Lubbock. It wasn't even windy; it looked perfect. I stared through the window, wondering what I should do for the day. It was a Saturday and this weekend I had no intention of going to the Department.

Looking to make some breakfast, I opened the refrigerator, but it was almost empty. I read the morning paper with black coffee and unbuttered toast. The guilt of not making use of such a good day finally started to bother me. I put the paper aside and looked through the window as though to assure myself the weather hadn't suddenly turned foul. I thought I should give Anu a call and see if she had any plans for the day.

I did not get Anu. Instead it was Amul who picked up her phone.

"We are thinking of cycling to the park on the southwest side of Loop 289. You know, take advantage of the weather. Do you want to join us? I could borrow someone's bike for you," offered Amul.

"Isn't that the park where the Indian Association of Lubbock is having their spring picnic party next Saturday?" I asked.

He said yes and invited me again to go cycling with them. I felt I might be intruding, so I made up an excuse. I suggested we could meet up at Student Body later that evening.

"Ok, we'll see you there at seven," said Amul and hung up.

I was just about to call Goops when I got a call from Nita. She told me there was going to be a pick up cricket game starting in about an hour at the soccer field near the Women's Gym. I was not good at cricket, but agreed to play anyway.

"Hey, I would also like to talk to you about something after the game," she said, as though it was an after thought.

I told her that I was meeting up with Amul and Anu in the evening and she could join us there to talk about what she had on her mind.

"What time are they supposed to meet you?"

"Amul said seven."

"Ok, can you meet me there like half an hour earlier?" she asked.

"Sure, I'll see you soon by the Women's Gym," I said and hung up.

"There's a spot open on Team India. You can take that," said Dave as I got to the field near the Women's Gym.

I looked around the field. The game had already started and I realized what Dave was talking about. It was the Indian students vs. the Rest of the World. I could see West Indians, Pakistanis, Bangladeshis, English, and Australians scattered around the field. It looked like India was batting. I asked Nita, who seemed to be the self appointed cheerleader of the Indian team, what the score was. She laughed.

"You only missed four balls of the first over and we have lost two wickets. But this guy Rahul you see there— he'll pull us through—he knocked a 4 and a 6!"

She went back to her cheerleading and I strolled over to Dave who was fielding not too far from where I was standing.

"In case you are wondering," he said with a wink, "I appointed myself as the match coordinator and captain of the Rest of the World team."

"I'm sure everyone appreciates that Dave," I said. He laughed and slapped me on the back.

Just then there was some loud cheering on the field. Rahul's wicket had just fallen and the West Indian wicket keeper was tossing the middle stump in the air.

The hot shower felt good after the cricket game. I dressed up and looked at the time. It was only getting to be 6 o'clock. I debated what I should do. Nita wouldn't be at Student Body for another half an hour. I decided I'd go anyway and have a drink by myself while I waited for her.

There weren't many people in the bar. It was too early for a Saturday night I thought. I walked toward the bar counter. The bartender knew me, so he already had my beer waiting on the counter. Suddenly I felt something hit my back. I turned around and saw Nita taking aim at me again with an ice cube.

"Hey, I thought you said 6:30," I said.

"Yeah, but can't a girl have a drink by herself?" she asked in mock surprise.

I put my beer on the table and pulled a chair near her. She motioned the bartender for a refill of her drink.

"What you having?" I asked.

"Gin," she replied.

"Listen, let me get to the point before Anu and Amul come," she said taking a generous sip of the gin.

"I am looking for a relationship. And I want it soon," she blurted out.

I was taken aback, but tried to put on a straight face. "Just for the sake of a relationship?"

"No, but I feel I'm ready."

I didn't know what to say, so I reached for my beer glass. "Actually, I know I should explain more," she said.

"You know I'm getting old, way old by Indian standards for a girl to remain single. You know that. But here's the thing...last couple of months my parents have been asking me to fly back to Singapore and you know... they want to fix me up with this guy—some successful

115

Rajastani business guy or something - they know over there."

She took another generous sip of her gin and looked at me. I reached for my beer glass.

"Now, don't think I haven't told them I am not for arranged married and all that. But they just don't seem to understand. You understand, right?"

She didn't wait for me to answer.

"But I don't want to get into a fight with them over this. They are my parents, right?"

This time she paused and so I replied.

"Why not, it is your future and life you are talking about. You can't back down on this issue so as to avoid a fight with your parents. I mean its marriage we are talking about for Christ's sake."

The door to the bar opened and we both looked reflexively to see if it was Amul and Anu. But it wasn't. It was two guys dressed like cowboys, complete with eight gallon hats, tight blue jeans, and chewing tobacco. There was a girl with them too. Almost as tall as them, but she was dressed pretty normal, which I thought was a little odd.

"I know that Thomas, I know, but that's precisely why I want to find a relationship," said Nita.

"So as to avoid a fight with your parents?"

"You're impossible!" said Nita with some irritation.

"I was only rationalizing from what you said," I said.

"And that's exactly why you don't have a woman in your life," she said.

I looked into my glass. There wasn't much beer left. I drank what was left, gestured to Nita that I was going to get a refill and got up.

"I'm sorry...I didn't mean it that way," she said apologetically.

"Do you want another gin?" I asked.

The two guys dressed like cowboys were standing by the counter. They nodded at me and I returned the acknowledgement. The bartender got me a fresh glass of beer and a glass of gin and tonic.

I pulled the chair next to Nita and put the drinks on the table.

"I want to get to know somebody and marry him. I don't believe in the Indian system. I'm not doing it to avoid a fight with my parents. I want to do it for me. I owe it to me."

She stirred her gin with a plastic straw looking into the glass.

"But it seems to me you are looking for a relationship only because your parents brought the pressure on. I just think if you were really ready for it, you would have found love by now. You can force this if you want to Nita, but it might not turn out right. It will be just an arranged marriage, except that you arranged it for yourself, instead of your parents," I said.

She looked at me and I moved my eyes away slowly from direct eye contact. I felt like I needed a cigarette. I got up and turned around to go to the bar counter, and I saw Amul and Anu coming toward our table. I felt happy to see them. I looked at my wristwatch. It was 7 o'clock.

I looked outside through the window of the living room just before I stepped out of my apartment. It looked like another clear spring day. But it wasn't the weather I was checking this Saturday; it was for Goops' car. He had offered to give me a ride to the park where the Indian Association of Lubbock was holding their annual spring picnic. The Indian students were always invited every year to this event, except one year sometime in the distant past, I was told. No one actually remembered, or preferred not to remember, why that happened, but there was vague mention of an Indian male student making an indecent proposal to the daughter of a prominent Indian in the association.

The dust rose from the parking lot of the apartment as Goops brought his black Escort GT to an abrupt stop. I noticed his license plate had expired and made a mental note to remind him.

"Yeah, I'm going to get to it," said Goops, as he got out of the car, with his usual grin, as though he read the mental note I just made.

"I always get that look on my car," he added with his characteristic grin.

I got in the car and we drove on the Loop until we got to the park. Goops parked the car and we walked toward the place where we saw some Indian families.

"Here take these *samosas*...they are vegetarian only," said Mrs. Jha as she handed a bowl full of *samosas* to Goops and me. We politely took a *samosa* each and helped ourselves to canned beer, which was immersed in a large

119

metal bucket with ice that was now all nearly melted. Before we opened our cans we saw Mrs. Jha drop the *samosa* bowl on the table and run toward a boy who was probably six years old. The boy appeared to be her son. We saw her stoop to his eye level and it seemed she was scolding him for rolling his shirtsleeve above his elbow.

"Your hands will become dark," she admonished him as she pulled his sleeves down and buttoned them.

"Now go play," she said.

We moved around the picnic area making small talk with people we knew. We finally settled in a small group where a couple of students were standing around with a can of beer or soft drink in their hands, just like us.

"You cannot deny the freedom of choice this country offers! My God, how can you even compare it with India?"

It was Dr. Mathew's voice. It was his reaction to something Goops had said, which I wasn't paying much attention to, while standing around the small group of people. I had met Dr. Mathew on a couple of occasions before. I knew that he had emigrated from India in the late sixties and did some specialization in medicine in

Wisconsin, moved to Lubbock, and set up a very lucrative practice.

"I think you are missing the point I just made Doctor. I am not denying that there is a lack freedom of choice in the US. All I'm saying is in reality a lot of that is perceived. Sure, in theory it's there..."

I looked away, not paying attention, and not wanting to get into some intellectual argument. Not when the weather was this good. It was perfect weather for a picnic. I could see four and five year olds kicking a soccer ball far from where we were standing. Many of the Indian women where sitting on the grass near where their kids where kicking around the soccer ball. I could also see Dr. Raman trying to persuade some of the women to play volleyball.

"See let me tell you this Young Man," I heard Dr. Mathew say. "You can become anything you want in this country. But you have to be prepared to work hard. They don't care who or what you are here, as long as you do a good job, your success is mostly guaranteed. It's what this country is all about, Young Man. And you should learn to appreciate it. For your own good."

"Just because things worked out for you doesn't mean everyone has the opportunity you are talking about. Do you know how many people like you actually make it to have this American dream? There are so many people in this country who work very hard, but all they get is a nickel or a dime. Shit, millions of them don't have basic health insurance, no education, not enough money, and there's very little hope they can break out of this poverty. A lot of them are minorities or poor whites, which doesn't help. And these people work hard, Doctor, doing all sorts of work that you and me don't even know what it takes," said Goops restraining his voice from sounding as if he was shouting.

"How much freedom of choice do they and their kids have, Doctor?" asked Goops raising his voice.

"Who are these people you are talking about, Son?" asked Dr. Mathew with a contemptuous grin looking at everyone in the group. I turned my head away.

I looked to where I had seen Dr. Raman. I was curious to know about his success on getting the women to play volleyball with him. It now looked like he had found some success. I could see several women, in attires not exactly suited for volleyball, trying to make contact with the ball.

"Well let's start with immigrants like you. I'm sorry they don't have an M.D. But a lot of them work 10 or 14 hours a day...earning minimum wage. They have kids to feed and clothe. And on minimum wage, how the hell are they ever going to move up on the food chain. They have no choice but to keep showing up for their minimum wage job for the rest of their lives. No riches, Doctor. No dream. No choice that you talk about. And guess what...nobody wants to increase the minimum wage because I suspect if they do people in your socio-economic class couldn't milk so much out of this country..."

It was Goops. He had started to raise his voice. I stopped watching the success of Dr. Raman's pick up volleyball game and turned my attention back to the argument Goops was having with Dr. Mathew.

"Are you communist?" asked Dr. Mathew in a firm voice, as though he had follow-up questions ready to be fired as soon as Goops answered.

"Are you a bourgeois?" shot back Goops.

"Young man, I didn't come to this country with riches. I had nothing but a dream of making something out of myself."

"And I bet they admitted you at Wisconsin for an M.D. based on this dream," said Goops sarcastically, looking around the group as if to garner support for his argument. But the two people in the group besides me, who were also students, just smiled as though they were uninterested in the argument or did not want to say anything impolite to the doctor. Goops looked at me then. I felt a little uncomfortable with the tone Goops' voice had taken in the argument. But I knew he was passionate about his opinions.

"I agree with Gopal, Doctor," I said.

"The truth of the matter I think is you can make it big in this country, if you already have an asset, like specialized education in your case. Of course you will read about the average Jose, or Anandamurthy, Chang, or Murphy who came to this country with five bucks in their pockets and made it five hundred thousand or five million bucks. But the sad fact is they are probably only 1% of them. The rest are probably sweating it out for five bucks an hour and will sweat it out like that for the rest of their lives. And don't tell me there is no other country that people don't make it from rags to moderate riches like you did," said Goops.

"Then why didn't you gentlemen go to those other countries?" asked Dr. Mathew contemptuously.

"The GDP," said Goops without hesitation.

The two students who were politely smiling now started to laugh. But from the tone of their laugh it wasn't hard to say if they were leaning toward Goops or Dr. Mathew.

"You can deny the choices you have here if you want Young Man, but now let me tell you this interesting story," said Dr. Mathew, now addressing the two students who were laughing.

"See when my sister was getting married in India," Dr. Mathew continued.

"My parents looked for a suitable boy who was a doctor, a lawyer, or an engineer." He slapped his thigh laughing animatedly.

"That is how much choice she had in getting a husband. But in America you can marry anyone you want. There are no half-baked caste based nonsensical notions here. Nobody arranges marriages for you. You marry who you want. You make the choice because you have the choice," said Dr. Mathew. He was looking at Goops as he said the last sentence.

I looked away before he looked at me. I felt the cool spring breeze against my cheeks. I looked to see how the volleyball game was doing. I could see the women Dr. Raman had recruited to play were all laughing, although I could not hear them from where I was standing. I looked at them again and felt happy to see the men and the women all playing together with their children, who were also playing near them. The trees behind them were partly green and even the weeds sticking out of the mowed grass of the park had a certain appeal in spring. But I was here with Dr. Mathew and Goops in an argument; not there with the men, women, children and the green trees and the weeds. I felt a desire to be there with them, not just be there with them, but be one of them. But then I thought of what Nita had said of me in the bar. I wondered if I would ever be one of them.

Dr. Mathew was waving his hands frantically, as if he was protesting something Goops was saying. But Goops did not allow him to interrupt.

"That's exactly my point. Most whites marry whites. Most blacks marry blacks. Most Hispanics marry Hispanics. Most Asians marry their own kind. Most rich marry their own kind, and most professionals marry other professionals in America. And like you said, all sorts of people marry all sorts of people, but again they are a tiny minority. And you can't deny it's more than eyebrows raised and prejudice involved in interracial marriages, or when a doctor marries a construction worker. It mostly doesn't happen in America. The perceived choice is there, but people look for their own kind to get married to. Not so much of a choice — it's a perceived choice. So odds are even if your sister was here, she would have found a doctor, or a lawyer, or an engineer and an Indian one too. The few that do cross over the boundary - that does happen in India too. You know that, or have you forgotten?"

It was Goop replying to what Dr. Mathew had said.

Dr. Mathew was not laughing now. The two other students were not either. Goops did not look at me for support this time. But Dr. Mathew did.

"You may think you have a choice in your mind, but if you arrange your own marriage, it's still an arranged marriage, Doctor," I said.

127

CHAPTER 10

The Politics of Love

It had stopped snowing in Toronto. It was a clear Tuesday afternoon as Mammen briefly checked his pocket map and walked toward Simcoe Street. The snow had been cleared from the sidewalks leading to the consulate, but it had not been removed from the sidewalks, only swept to the side. There was no line at the consulate gates as Mammen approached the building. He sighed in relief. The thought of standing in line as he had last Friday morning, in temperatures below zero, was still vivid in his memory. Not that it was anywhere nearly as cold as that today. A guard at the gates of the consulate accosted him.

"I'm here to pick up my passport and visa," said Mammen as he showed his ticket.

The guard nodded and waved him into the building.

Inside the building there was a line leading to the counter where passports were being handed back. Up ahead in the line Mammen noticed Gundu Rao. Strangely, Mammen felt happy to see Gundu Rao. He thought it must be because he not seen a familiar face since last Friday. The nervousness he had felt on Friday was absent today. Mammen knew he had his visa approved—the burly black visa officer had told him that last Friday—all he had to do now was wait patiently in line and get his passport back with the visa stamped in it and then go back to the States. He thought of the journey that he had taken to get to this point. Now it would only be a few more minutes in the line and then the dream he had when he came as a student to America five years ago, would be realized. He thought Gundu Rao must also be feeling the same way, but then on second thoughts maybe not. Maybe Gundu Rao felt the visa he was going to get as a natural entitlement, which he deserved, for after all he was working for Goodyear. Mammen suspected Gundu Rao had had the easier route to get to this line and therefore could not appreciate this moment the way he, Mammen, could. To Mammen,

129

Gundu Rao did not seem like one who had gone through the same financial struggles that he, like so many foreign graduate students, go through. But then again, thought Mammen in consolation, Gundu Rao probably never made the same bond of friendship that people who struggle together often do.

He thought of the parties in run down apartments, like Sundown, which he never thought of as run down, until he moved to New York with a job. He remembered the night he had watched Amul dancing, Anu laughing with him, seeing Amita for the first time and reading her palm. It was two years ago, but somehow it didn't seem that long.

It had been oppressively hot in Lubbock that summer. It was late summer in the afternoon as I walked on Avenue X and turned to 8th Street. It was only about two months ago, I thought, that I was enjoying the cool breeze of spring on my cheeks at the park where the Indian Association held their annual spring picnic.

"Over here!" shouted Goops as I opened the creaking metallic gate of Sundown apartments. He was waving to me from an apartment on the ground floor.

I didn't know whose apartment it was, but seeing Goops standing at the doorway I wondered if the party had been moved from the apartment on the third floor.

"Naaa...they just got beer up there. But I organized some real booze for some select folks...you know what I'm saying?" grinned Goops when I asked him if there had been a change in venue for the party.

"Single malt?" I asked.

"However did you guess?" asked Goops pretending to be surprised.

Sometimes it was easy to forget that Goops, unlike the rest of us, had a lot of money, which he spent without any reservation. I took the glass of the single malt whiskey he served me and took a sip. Someone offered me some fried chicken drumsticks that were generously covered with Indian spices. I took a piece and squeezed lemon on it. It still tasted very spicy, but I thought that after a few drinks it might taste all right or if it didn't I wouldn't realize it.

"Next in line!" shouted the woman behind the counter. Mammen walked up to the counter and slipped the ticket, he had earlier shown the guard, through a slot under the glass window. She did not smile. She looked at the number on the ticket, searched through the stack of passports in front of her, pulled a blue colored one out and slipped it under the glass to Mammen in a very routine manner.

Mammen carefully verified the details on the visa that was stamped on his passport. Everything looked all right. He double-checked every detail. Then he carefully put the passport in a compartment of his shoulder bag and walked out of the consulate. Outside he saw Gundu Rao, as though he had been waiting for Mammen.

"I saw you in line and thought I would catch up with you," said Gundu Rao.

Mammen smiled.

"So what company do you work for in New York?" asked Gundu Rao bluntly.

Daylight had almost disappeared as more people came to Sundown Apartments. They were scattered from the ground floor all the way to the third floor, which was the actual location of the party. Almost all the Indian students I knew seemed to be there. Even Reena, Dave's Indian girlfriend who rarely socialized with Indians, had come. Not far from her I saw Dave laughing and talking with others. He seemed to be more comfortable with the Indian students than did Reena, who looked very out of place. The only reason she had come, it seemed to me, was because Dave had come.

"You will have to dance with me later. You missed the party last summer, so no excuses this time," said Amita looking at me as soon as she had kissed Goops, who was standing next to me. Goops and I were watching people coming through the creaky metallic gate.

I was hoping to see Anu coming through the gates, but didn't. Nor did I see Amul. I asked Amita if she knew, but she shrugged her shoulders and then seeing some of her friends call her from the third floor, left us.

I could hear the music coming alive from the third floor. It sounded as though it was coming from some cheap speakers like the ones you hear in bus stations in India. It was some popular Hindi movie song. But no one seemed to care about the quality of the speakers. People were singing along and I could tell by the way they were singing that they were very happy. But of course it could have also been the alcohol, I mused to myself.

Goops was going to get me another glass of single malt, but I declined. I thought I should head up to the third floor, meet some people and have a beer. I climbed the concrete staircase, bantering with people who were

133

standing along the staircase. Prashant was one of them. He seemed to be complaining. It was something about the money he was making as a research assistant. He smiled when he saw me, and I smiled back shaking my head and gestured to him that I wasn't going to be part of his audience. I passed the second floor and was on the first flight to the third floor when I saw Nita coming down the stairs. I stopped to talk to her. We greeted each other, but she didn't seem to have time to talk to me. She said she was in a hurry.

"I'll see you later," she said and hurried down.

I reached the third floor. I meandered through the people in the apartment and helped myself to a beer. There was a collection box on the table where I picked up the beer. I put in a few dollars in the box.

"I didn't see you come up," I said to Anu. She was standing in the kitchen of the apartment on the third floor with Mammen, Roberto, and Gabriella.

She smiled at me, but her eyes looked as though she had been crying. Roberto and Gabriella did not say anything when I looked at them, as though they were going to explain something to me, even without me asking them anything.

"Has Amul talked to you?" asked Anu.

"No."

"Well…" she began and looked away from all of us.

"Come on guys, let's go and ruffle Reena a bit. I hear she is here," said Mammen to Roberto and Gabriella. They seemed to have got the hint and quickly obliged.

After they left, Anu said, "Let's go outside and get some air."

We walked out of the apartment, but there were too many people singing there, so we walked down one floor and found a spot by the rails that were facing 8th Street. We leaned against the rails. There was a little breeze blowing against our faces. We stood there saying nothing. After a while she asked me how my plan to graduate in the fall was coming along. I was a little surprised, but replied, without sounding surprised, that it was mostly on track.

"We talked to our parents. It didn't go well," said Anu.

"But he is an upper caste Hindu like you," I said.

"But I am a Brahmin," she said, "And my parents have strong feelings about that."

"How about his parents?"

135

"They are OK with it, except I don't speak his language, which they are not too thrilled about. But I must say they are willing to talk."

"You are a Brahmin."

"You know I don't care about all that."

"I know. And his parents seem at least OK with it. I'm sure you and Amul must have half expected this. So why the tears?"

"Its Amul," she said wiping tears from her cheeks.

"I'm sorry," I said.

She shook her head as if to say it was okay.

"I don't have a problem going against the will of my parents. I thought we both knew that even though we hadn't openly discussed this issue. He says since his parents are not very happy and since my parents won't even accept him...he thinks its better we go our separate ways. He also said Indian marriages are marriages between families and not just..."

She did not complete her sentence. But she was not crying. She was just looking straight ahead into the night. We stood there for some more time saying nothing. I did not know what to say. Anything I could think of I knew it was the obvious and she must have already considered it.

So I just looked down below the rails. I saw Goops was still standing there near the gate where I had left him earlier. There were more people with him now and occasionally we could hear laughter from them. They could not see us because we were standing in the dark.

"I never expected him to say that," said Anu.

"And I feel there is something else bothering him...it's not just the issue with the parents," she continued after a pause.

"What do you mean?" I asked.

"I should not say it. It's not fair on him if I say it, because maybe it's not true and I am just imagining it," she said.

"Look Anu," I said, finally being able to string my thoughts together.

"He has been under a lot of stress because of Priya. I have noticed that he is struggling with himself ever since she came to the U.S. I first sensed this when I talked to him at the Student Body last fall. You remember when you and Roberto were arguing about multiculturalism...yeah, it was that day I thought he was having a hard time reconciling what he thought his ideas were and what they really are. I guess we are all confronted sooner or later with some situation in life that makes us question what we think of our outlook on life is and what it really is. When the two don't meet, we realize we are a bit phony...we realize the hollowness in the lofty idealism we talk about...and it's hard swallowing that. And for Amul I think that situation was his sister, Priya, coming and exploring her freedom in America and with it testing the limits of her brother's idealism that he had taken for granted. Either she went beyond the boundary of his idealism or maybe he realized his boundaries are far narrower than he thought. And it's hard to swallow that. You try to fight it, trying to convince yourself otherwise. But sooner or later you start suspecting that you are avoiding the truth," I said.

"And Priya eloping with an American didn't help," said Anu as though she was agreeing with me.

"I thought he came to terms with that," I said.

"I think he did, but his parents still haven't and that's what he has not come to terms with," she said.

We didn't say anything for a while. Then I asked, "So have you guys decided on what you two are going to do?"

"Nothing much, except that we will keep things as though nothing has happened and keep talking...I guess that is the only way we can resolve this without breaking our hearts any more…"

I saw tears slowly running down her cheeks. She didn't make any attempt to wipe them off. I looked away down to the where the people were standing around Goops. But the crowd was no more there. Even Goops had left. The only people I saw by the gate were two people leaving the party.

"I don't think Priya would have eloped had Amul been more acceptable to the idea that Brian was American. But I don't know…maybe he really did feel that it was not right for her to be getting into a relationship so soon and lose focus on why she came to America," I said.

"I know its easy for me to say that we will keep things as though nothing has happened and keep talking…but I know it cannot be the same again…I don't think its possible. I guess it's just like you said about confronting the truth about yourself, sooner or later. Either we accept that our parents are not going to accept this and get married or we just…" said Anu.

"You should give it time. Don't rush into any decision, Anu. There's politics in everything in life, Anu, even in love," I said.

"It is the one thing I thought was free from it," she said.

Anu wanted to get away from the party, so we walked to a coffee shop. It would have been a quicker to walk from Avenue X, but we wanted to avoid walking on Avenue X at night so we walked all the way to University Avenue and then trekked our way to the coffee shop on 19th Street. The night was cooler than it had been a few hours ago. There was a little breeze too. We walked side by side without saying much. I tried to change the subject of what we had been talking about on the second floor with more mundane topics. But I soon realized it was not going to take her mind away from what she was thinking about. So we walked silently until we got to the coffee shop.

The waitress was cheerful and she seated us as soon as we told her we just wanted coffee and nothing to eat. I had not come to this coffee shop in a long while, but used to frequent it in my first year in Lubbock because my then roommate, Vivek, would frequent this place and would persuade me to go along with him every now and then. It was always tempting to give in to Vivek's persuasions, because he would inevitably bring up a topic of logic after a few cups of coffee and we would argue into the early hours

140

of the morning. Thoroughly exhausted and happy we would walk back to our apartment, neither of us conceding defeat on most occasions. I was thinking about those days, and forgot that I was sitting with Anu.

The waitress brought a jug of coffee and two cups. I poured the coffee into both the cups and pushed one to Anu. Anu emptied four sugar packets into her cup and stirred it slowly.

"I am a liberal although I am a Brahmin. It is the liberal part of me that I think is at the root of what is bothering Amul. I think Priya made him aware, like you said, to confront his perception of himself and how liberal he wants his wife to be. What he can live with. It's not that he is worried I will behave like Priya in any way, but through her he realized that his boundaries are narrower than he lead himself to believe," she said, still stirring her coffee.

"Now I am wondering if inside me I am just a Brahmin after all and the liberal part of me is only the lofty perception of myself. One day I too may have to confront the truth and in the confrontation...who knows...I may realize I too have narrower boundaries than I perceived I had. That I'm just a phony liberal."

141

"But it's not you who is walking away from the marriage," I said.

"I know. But what if he was the Brahmin and I was him and it was his parents who would not accept me?" she asked.

"You can only be who you are and hope you come out all right when the confrontation happens," I said.

We looked out of the window. It had begun to rain lightly. We sat there saying nothing to each other. We just watched it rain. I looked at my watch. It was getting close to eleven o'clock. I thought of asking her if it was getting late for her and if she wanted to walk back to the party at Sundown, or if she just wanted to go home. I looked at her and saw she was still watching the rain and looked as though she was at peace with herself. So I did not say anything.

CHAPTER 11

An Autumn Remembered

The astronaut was floating in the dark emptiness that surrounded him. He was floating away from his ship and I could see him tug his life support cord, which had accidentally detached from the ship. As I watched him, it seemed he was trying to float back toward the ship, but the ship only got further away from him. He had appeared calm through all this, though it was hard to tell because of the bulky space suit that he was wearing. Then he started to wave his arm and his legs frantically. Now it wasn't hard to tell that he was no longer calm. Strangely I saw him float toward me. I wondered who he was. I peered through his visor. I saw two terrified eyes and through his eyes I saw a fetus tugging at its umbilical cord, which was separated from its mother. The next moment the fetus was floating in the dark empty space much like the astronaut I had seen earlier. Then I saw the fetus float toward me and its eyes opened abruptly. I looked at them and saw it was me.

I looked at my watch as I wiped the sweat off my forehead with the sleeve of my T-shirt, sitting up on the makeshift bed I was sleeping on. I could still see the eyes of the fetus from the dream I had just woken up from. It was past 4:30 in the morning. I fell back on the makeshift bed, but it was useless; I could not get back to sleep. I got up and without turning on the lights of the bedroom, I found my way to the kitchen. I was staying at the apartment of my friend and I did not want to disturb him or his roommate so early in the morning. I slowly turned the tap of the kitchen sink and filled a paper cup, that I found near the sink, with cold water and gulped it down.

I peered through the partially open blinds of the window by the sink and saw the fluorescent street lamps shining on 11th Street. It was empty. I thought of the countless times I had walked on 11th Street when I had been a student in Lubbock four years ago. I had never seen it so empty, or at least never remembered seeing it so empty.

144

But it was hardly five o'clock in the morning, I thought. And it wasn't four years ago.

It was four years since I had left Lubbock. I hadn't been entirely truthful to Anu at the party at Sundown that fall when she had asked me if my plans for graduation were on track. I had told her yes, not because I wanted to lie, but at the time I wanted to believe I could and had convinced myself so. When that fall came to an end and the first snow fell in Lubbock, I had still not completed my doctoral program. But I had a job offer from a company on the east coast. I had convinced myself that since I had completed all my research and analysis, all I had to do was to write up my thesis and this could be done while I worked on the east coast. My advisor and chairman thought otherwise. But I was confident I could do this, so I took up the job offer and left Lubbock without completing my thesis and thus not earning my Ph.D. The prospect of earning real money was too tempting to pass up.

Then three years passed, but I had not written a single sentence for my thesis, until one day while going through my mail I saw an envelope with the university seal. Thinking it was from the alumni association I did not bother opening it immediately. Days later while cleaning

145

my desk I came across the envelope again and opened it. It wasn't from the alumni association. It was from the office of the graduate school. I read the two paragraph letter over and over again. It was a friendly reminder that time was running out to defend my thesis, and in light of that, I had to defend no later than the end of the year, or forfeit the privilege to earn my Ph.D. The effect of the letter on me was immediate. I was not about to lose my Ph.D after four years of research I had put in, just because I didn't write up my thesis. Not after four years at Lubbock. So every night for the next six months I religiously worked on putting my thesis together. Several revisions later, the graduate school accepted my thesis and set a date for my defense.

That date for my defense was the day I stood in front of the window by the kitchen sink and watched the emptiness of 11th Street at five in the morning. I was nervous and perhaps a little terrified of facing my doctoral committee. They had the power to pass or fail me and I knew my four years of absence wouldn't be looked upon kindly. It was this nervousness that triggered the dream about the astronaut and the fetus, I thought, trying to make sense of the dream. But somehow I felt my rationalization of the dream was not convincing and it bothered me.

I walked away from the window and sat on the couch in the living room. There was only darkness, save for the distant streetlights on 11th Street, that made its way into the room through the partially open blinds of the kitchen window. And it was very quiet. I felt as though I was alone in the apartment.

I did not see Anu many more times after the night we had sat at the coffee shop and watched the rain. She had become withdrawn after she and Amul had decided to go their separate ways. She graduated that fall with a master's in chemical engineering and moved to the Baltimore area. We kept in touch for about a year since that fall, but then she moved to Brazil, abandoning her career in chemical engineering. I did not hear from her for a long time after that. Then one morning two years later she called me over the phone and we talked for a long time. She said she was working for a non-profit social services organization in Sao Paulo. She sounded very happy over the phone and I mentioned that to her. She sounded very effervescent like the days when she wrote the controversial article in the *University Times*. I asked her in jest if anyone in Sao Paulo had attempted to break her arm yet. She laughed and then turned serious. She said that night we sat in the coffee shop

147

and watched the rain, she started thinking on what she wanted to do with the rest of her life.

My thesis defense was only at three o' clock in the afternoon. But it was barely past five in the morning and I was restless. I sat on the couch not knowing what to do. I got up and walked to the window by the kitchen sink and looked out again. There were signs of life now, with pickup trucks passing by every now and then.

I had kept in touch with Amul for a while after I had left Lubbock four years ago. He still had a semester to complete when I had left. He too, like Anu, had become withdrawn, but unlike Anu I felt something fundamentally had changed in him. His attitude toward life changed, I thought, although I couldn't exactly put a finger on what exactly had changed in him. But he was not so much of a free thinker anymore as he had been. When I did talk to him over the phone from the east coast he would talk to me about his sister Priya. He still felt as though Priya had wronged him and his family by eloping and getting married. But then after a few months he would not even mention her when I talked to him. By then he had graduated and had started working in Silicon Valley. His topic of conversation was all about his work and the pressure that came with working for a start up software company. Each time I talked to him I got the impression he wanted to move away from his memories of Lubbock and some of those memories included me. I stopped calling him and thought it best to let him call me if wanted to keep in touch. He never did.

It was with Mammen that I still had contact, although not very frequently. About two years ago he sent me an e-mail describing his trip to Toronto to the U.S. consulate to get his visa. He too, like Amul, was working for a software company in New York. About six months after that e-mail I got an invitation card for his wedding. He later called me over the phone to extend a personal invitation. Apparently his parents had arranged a marriage for him. He said his fiancée was also a software programmer like him. I asked him if he had kept in touch with any of our common friends from the Lubbock days. He told me about how he ran into Amita about a year ago in New York City. She was visiting her relatives in the Bronx. He said they talked for many hours and he complained to her that he did not get a wedding invitation either from her or Goops. She said she and Goops had broken up soon after they left Lubbock, but she wouldn't say what had happened between them and Mammen did not press. She did say something that surprised Mammen though.

"You knew all along, that Goops and I wouldn't get married didn't you," she had said to Mammen.

"Why would you say that?" Mammen had asked.

"Well, remember the party at Sundown one summer when I met you for the first time?"

"Yes."

"Do you remember reading Goops and my palm?"

"Yes, but I didn't say anything...I didn't say anything...I remember saying the light was not enough to read your palms."

"I know you didn't say anything Mammen, except that the light was not enough."

"And I didn't even look up."

"Yes, you didn't even look up. And that's why I knew. You were afraid your eyes would betray what you saw in my palms if you looked up at me."

I asked Mammen if what she said was true, but he avoided the question.

Before he put the phone down, Mammen said to me,

"Oh, by the way, Dave and Reena got married. I visited them in Dallas when I went there on business. They bought a house in the Arlington area. They seem to be very happy together."

I talked to Mammen only a couple of times after that. I had called him when he got back to the U.S. after his wedding. In the last call I had made to him he seemed content with married life and kept talking about how things had changed in his life and how priorities had changed and how he "had moved on." The way he talked it was as if he wanted me to read between the lines that I should "move on" as well.

As for Nita, I never heard from her directly after I left Lubbock. But I had heard through Anu that she had got married and settled in Houston. I was curious to know if she had found her love that she seemed to desperately want or if she yielded to her parents' wishes and married the man they picked for her. I asked Anu about it when she called me, but Anu did not know.

I waited outside the conference room on the fourth floor of the Department, not far from the lecture room in which I had lectured so many times as a substitute for my professor. My committee had asked me to wait outside for a few minutes after I had completed my thesis defense. But it was now close to twenty minutes since I had been waiting and they had not called me back. I felt uneasy. Had they found a hole in my thesis? Would they require me to do more work on it? Would they fail me? I tried not thinking about the worst. To distract my thoughts I walked up to the large windows opposite the conference room that overlooked the main entrance to the department.

I looked below and saw people walking going in and out of the building. It appeared as though they were moving aimlessly, as if they were lost. But I soon realized it was my uneasiness and fear that I was projecting on them. I turned back and looked at the door of the conference room expecting it to open any moment. But the door remained closed. I walked to the door and peered through the small window on the door. I saw my committee members listening to the professor from the mathematics department who had been assigned to observe my thesis by the graduate school. It was always these mathematicians who didn't understand what engineers did, I thought, already concluding that the mathematics professor was raising objections to something in my research.

I turned back and walked to the large windows. Just then I heard the door of the conference room open. I turned back and saw my chairman smile.

It was getting dark when I walked out of the Department's main entrance. I thought about the importance of this day—I was no more a doctoral student. I had earned my doctorate. But I could not feel any emotions in me. I kept walking, not exactly sure where I should go, but I was getting away from the Department and that's all that seemed to matter. I got to University Avenue and I crossed it to get to my friend's apartment where I had been staying for the past couple of days. I suddenly remembered Goops would be coming in soon from Midland, an oil town a couple of hours drive from Lubbock. He had been on assignment there with an oil services company for a year and when he heard I was coming to Lubbock for my defense, he said he would make time to come see me after work. He had said he would wait for me at the Student Body.

I crossed University Avenue and stood by a wooden bench on the sidewalk. I still felt the empty feeling in me. I felt like talking to Bafana and looked for the forked dust road that would lead me to Save the Children House.

153

Of course it was just fantasy. But I could smell the air of Maseru and the memories flooded me. I felt queasy, so I sat on the wooden bench. I wondered why I thought of Bafana and Maseru after so many years. My stomach was hurting. I thought of the night I had gone to see him after the *tsotsi* had tried to mug me. I recalled meeting Poone, who only smoked Gunston cigarettes. I recalled Bafana teasing me. I closed my eyes. And then I felt like the fetus that had been cut off from its mother.

I sat on the bench for a long time. I don't know how long I cried. It was now dark and I saw the neon sign of Student Body flickering from a distance. Goops must be waiting I thought and walked toward Student Body. I got to the door and looked inside through the window by the side of the door. I saw Goops perched on a barstool. I waited for a moment and then I turned the knob of the door.

About the Author

B. Thomas Kattapuram was born in India and was brought up in four African countries over sixteen years. He has since lived in India and the United States. Having been a foreigner most of his life he has keenly observed several cultures and peoples and the surprising similarity in thinking and behavior among them. It is based on this experience that he brings several everyday observations of these cultures to life through his characters in *A Close World Apart*. He digs deeper into the observations and provokes thought in the reader.

A Close World Apart is the author's first novel. Kattapuram has a Ph. D and resides in Michigan.